Jan Ken Po

Jan Ken Po
The World of Hawaii's
Japanese Americans

Dennis M. Ogawa

foreword by
Senator Daniel K. Inouye

The University Press of Hawaii
Honolulu

Library of Congress Cataloging in Publication Data

Ogawa, Dennis M.
  Jan ken po.

  Bibliography: p.
  1. Japanese Americans—Hawaii—Social life and customs. 2. Hawaii—Social life and customs.
I. Title.
DU624.7.J3I36   1978   301.45′15′20969   78-9513
ISBN 0-8248-0398-1

To Amy and Keiji

Contents

Foreword

As a person privileged to serve in the United States Senate, and as an American of Japanese ancestry, I have met a wide variety of people and read numerous books, articles, and reports dealing with a range of subjects. Many of these readings, not surprisingly, have discussed the Japanese American: the various aspects of the cultural, economic, and philosophical factors which make him the individual that he is.

Of these readings, *Jan Ken Po: The World of Hawaii's Japanese Americans* is one of the most refreshing and readable. It was written by a Japanese American from Hawaii who draws from his own experiences for the book's material. Because of this, *Jan Ken Po* can provide for the reader an excellent introduction to the Japanese American without the complexity of academic verbiage.

This book should serve to bring about a much better understanding of the how's and why's of the Japanese American—not only in terms of his historical experience, but also in how he probably sees his future. Writings like *Jan Ken Po* can foster better intercultural understanding, and in that way, foster the peace and tranquility that we all seek. I hope that similar books covering other ethnic groups will soon be forthcoming.

Daniel K. Inouye
United States Senator

Acknowledgments

Although my name appears on the front cover as the author, there are other individuals who have made valuable contributions toward the writing and development of this book. Margaret Yamate, Seymour Lutzky, and Katsumi Onishi provided editorial help during various stages in the development of this manuscript. Bert Sakuda and Marcella Barcelona gave critical suggestions on certain concepts presented in different chapters, and Jerry Fujioka and Eugene Fujioka compiled the photographs. Gratitude is also owed to Raymond Fujikawa for contributing the stories provided in chapter 7 and to his daughter, Sandy, whose charming photograph enhanced the cover of the original hardbound publication. I wish also to thank Glen Grant whose editorial and research skills as well as perceptive comments were invaluable in the preparation of this book. Finally, I must acknowledge the endearing patience of those closest to me, my wife, Amy, and son, Quin.

Research support for this book was provided by the Japanese American Research Center (JARC), sponsored by the Honolulu Japanese Chamber of Commerce, and a Rockefeller Foundation Grant through the American Studies Department at the University of Hawaii.

1
Acting Like One Japanee

Above the roar of model airplanes, nearby traffic and the noisy play of children and adults enjoying an afternoon in the park, the air is filled with the melodic sounds of Japanese music. From a loudspeaker secured in a *wiliwili* tree, you can hear the music of *"Tsuki ga deta deta,"* from the popular folksong *"Tanko Bushi."* At a curious gathering of Japanese Americans, young and old, a Nisei woman listens and starts to sing along. Her voice is not professional; it warbles and it occasionally sounds out of tune. But her spirit is genuine and the crowd of listeners applaud enthusiastically.

Sitting on *goza* mats neatly placed in the shade of a large *kamani* tree, three elderly Issei men tune their *shamisen,* an instrument like a banjo whose twangy sounds are so reminiscent of Japan. One player looks up, his seared face deeply tanned from his years of plantation work, to see a small Yonsei boy who stands close by, watching and listening as if hypnotized. The old Issei says something in Japanese and then laughs, revealing his shiny gold-capped front teeth.

The young boy stays to listen to the music from the *shamisen* for only a short while. Perhaps he is more interested in how the old men tune their instruments than in the harsh and unusual sounds which they produce. Perhaps he just can't understand the music. At any rate, he wanders away, eating his shave ice and walking among the many families who are sitting cross-legged around low tables loaded with food. The lunch which the families eat consists of such *gochisō,* good things to eat, as chicken or beef *teriyaki*-style, egg omelet rolled and cut into pieces, shrimp, fish or vegetable *tempura, musubi* with *ume* and *nori,* spam or vienna sausage, *takuan, namasu* and plenty of macaroni or potato salad.

A Nisei mother, wearing a straw hat with red and white stripes, reaches across a hot *hibachi* to turn over the sizzling *opelu,* Hawaiian fish. She asks her husband who is relaxing with friends and casually eating from his paper plate if he could call the children.

The father calls to his children who are at a large area outlined with small red flags attached to sticks planted in the ground. This area is the scene for the many games and races which have been arranged for this large picnic of Japanese American families. Using a microphone, the announcer, who speaks with a Japanese accent, is encouraging the children of a certain age group to get ready for the balloon-breaking contest. Ten youngsters finally line up at the starting point after some coaxing from their parents. The signal is given and they race across the course and then start to blow up a balloon. The first child who can blow up the balloon and make it pop by sitting on it wins.

A little later, ten Issei women paired into couples begin their race. Each couple has one of their feet in a

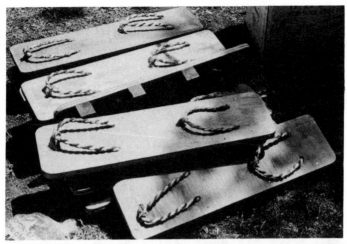

The Issei women use the double *geta* in their three-legged race. *Photo courtesy of Jerry Y. Fujioka, Light Inc.*

double *geta* and one foot free. In a manner similar to a three-legged race, the women move as fast as they can to outdistance their opponents. Though they don't maneuver very fast, revealing the stiffness in their spines, their bodies are responding to their souls and not their logic.

As these contests take place, a crowd of grandparents, parents and children are watching, shouting, encouraging, heckling and laughing. One race which is sure to produce laughter is the egg rolling contest, where Nisei men push raw eggs across the field with their noses. The spectators can rest assured that at least one contestant will emerge with the egg's yolk dripping from his face.

But win or lose, in each race prizes are given to all the contestants. From ten to twelve large cardboard boxes which contain fruits, vegetables, household goods,

The signal is given and the young children race across the course. *Photo courtesy of Eugene Y. Fujioka, Light Inc.*

school supplies or small toys, gifts are selected and distributed.

More prizes are given out after lunch when the "lucky number" drawing is held. Each person holds a numbered ticket given to him upon arrival. Parents give their tickets to the children who clamor around the announcer waiting for their numbers to be called. From a milk carton with the top cut off, a number is selected and announced over the microphone. The children rush

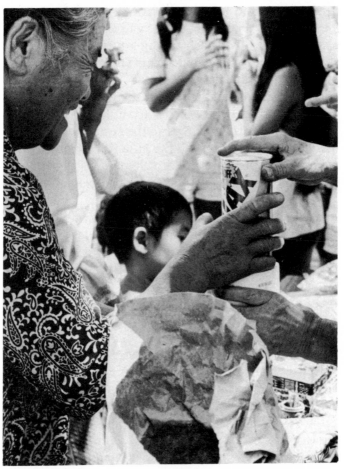

By the time each family leaves the picnic, everyone will have a gift to take home. *Photo courtesy of Jerry Y. Fujioka, Light Inc.*

up to receive the prizes won by their families: a bag of flour or sugar, canned goods, a box of kleenex, toilet paper, household items or linens. The grand prize for the day: a 100 pound bag of rice and a small kitchen appliance. By the time each family leaves on this Sunday afternoon, everyone will have a gift to take home.

After the drawings, the crowd begins to disperse. Some families remain in an area shaded by a large banyan tree which provides shelter from the hot sun. Some of their children wander over to the nearby canal. Using small nets they try to catch the little fish which they see swimming in the water. Other children go to get some more shave ice from the middle-aged Nisei man wearing a T-shirt with the words "Easy Brah" on the back. He stands behind an old green apparatus, turning a crank which grinds a block of ice into fine shavings. Still other children go to the nearby beach where they can dig in the sand and splash in the refreshingly cool saltwater of the dark blue lagoon.

On any Sunday during the summer months, if you walk across Ala Moana Park from where it begins near the Ala Wai Harbor to where it ends near Kewalo Basin, you will see the above scenes and many more, repeated from one group of Japanese American picnickers to another. Under each clump of trees, a white banner with bright letters suspended from ropes will declare the site of a different picnic sponsored by a different organization. Some of these gatherings are quite large, involving 400 to 500 people; others appear small in comparison with perhaps only 35 or 50 participants. Some have made elaborate preparations involving microphones, colorful pennants and lanterns, entertainment and a display of individual name signs which give recognition to those people who have donated money or

The youngest and the oldest generations of Japanese Americans enjoying a Sunday afternoon together. *Photo courtesy of Jerry Y. Fujioka, Light Inc.*

gifts; others are simple affairs without any extensively prearranged activities. At some picnics one is struck by the amount of time which must have been spent to prepare the foods; at others, rows and rows of small pink boxes indicate that the picnic is being catered.

In Hawaii there are many places where one sees a gathering of Japanese Americans: in the home for a family get-together, at the neighbors' for a backyard feast, or standing in line at the Nippon or Toyo theaters on a Friday evening or a Saturday morning. But no social event is more publicly revealing of Japanese

American life and culture than the Ken *(Kenjin Kai)* picnics held in parks and beaches throughout the Islands of Hawaii. Whether large or small, elaborate or simple, the Ken picnic to this day remains an important social activity.

Indeed, very rarely will a non-Japanese see the internal lives of the Japanese American more publicly exposed than at the Ken picnics. Here, for people to notice as they pass on tour buses or wander leisurely through the park, are the four major generations of Japanese Americans: Issei, Nisei, Sansei and Yonsei. Here are the favorite games and pastimes of a people which can easily be observed. Here are the more popular Japanese tunes and folksongs which still survive in the Japanese American culture, to be enjoyed and appreciated. Here are the foods and habits of a people which even the remotest onlooker could savor and relish. Here, in its many aspects and dimensions, in all its simplicity and complexity is the culture of the modern Japanese American of Hawaii.

Because it is so publicly known, the Ken picnic serves as a useful starting point to understanding Hawaii's Japanese Americans. But more than that, the Ken picnic is also illustrative of the current cultural status of this ethnic group. On the one hand, Ken picnics serve not only as a time of fun and conversation, but as a time to reaffirm the traces of Japanese culture which exist for the different generations, especially the Issei and Nisei. It is a time to reassure oneself that he is indeed a Japanese who has a common identity with other Japanese.

To explain this, it is necessary to state that the Ken picnics are arranged by and held for families that belong to Ken clubs. To belong to a Ken club, the member, the member's parents or grandparents must have originated from a specific area or prefecture in Japan. For example, the Kanegushiku Sonjin Kai is comprised of Issei who came from an area a few miles outside of Naha in Okinawa, and their descendants. Once each year, to re-establish the common ties to Japan, the Ken picnic is arranged. There the Issei can enjoy the comfort of relating to other Isseis with the same language mixture of pidgin English and Japanese. The Nisei, who come from distances as scattered as Kailua, Waipahu or Aiea, can renew friendships and acquaintances, get the latest news or simply gossip. The younger children use the Ken picnic as an opportunity to go to the beach, to play with their friends or to win prizes. At any rate, in the Ken picnics can be found a certain attachment of the Japanese Americans to their Japanese homeland and the influence of Japanese culture on their daily patterns and lifestyles.

But it would be amiss not to stress the fact that on the other hand, much of the Ken picnic has become "Americanized." The nature of the Ken clubs which before World War II was strictly limited to immigrants from common prefectures has given way to a more general and open format. For example, the Hiroshima Gōyū Kai became the Shinyū Aloha Kai after the war and membership rules were changed. Now only one spouse needs to have originated from Hiroshima Ken for a family to be accepted as members, instead of both. The erasure of strict Ken lines is also portrayed in the changes of membership requirements for a club which once consisted of university graduates of Kumamoto Ken lineage. Now any Japanese American university graduate is admitted regardless of Ken affiliation.

So a Sunday walk through Ala Moana Park would

reveal more kinds of Ken picnics than entailed in the strict notion of Japanese who share a common place of origin in Japan. The Hawaii Economic Study Club, the Kaimuki and Moiliili clubs, organizations geared not to Japanese background but circumstances in Hawaii, have altered the original intentions of the Ken picnics. Rather than only trying to rekindle affections for Japan, the picnics serve to bring Island communities or organizations closer together.

Moreover, one cannot help but be struck by the many non-Japanese aspects which have crept into the Ken picnic; time and progress have made a rural Japanese farmer's activity take on the gloss of American life. Participants park their cars in the modern Ala Moana Shopping Center then cross busy Ala Moana Boulevard to get to the picnic. Many bring buckets of chicken purchased from Kentucky Fried Chicken or bags of malasadas from Leonard's Bakery; many of the games are shared by all ethnic groups and are not of Japanese origin. Small transistor radios broadcast pop music or the Islander baseball game; teenage girls wear bikinis to go to the beach; teenage boys bring their surf boards. Most people wear Aloha shirts or T-shirts advertising this or that local business. The young people speak English or pidgin; they know little Japanese; they seem to ignore the Japanese music or simply tolerate it; they hardly seem to be finding any mystical bond with Japan.

To the tourist from Japan who will observe this strange phenomenon of cultural lifestyle in Ala Moana Park and to the *malihini* haole who may have just arrived from Iowa, something appears very curious about these people who are called Japanese Americans. They seem to show many of the same characteristics of living that each observer could find at home. But at the same time, they are different; they lack many of the distinguishable looks and behaviors necessary to be called a Japanese or an American. They seem strangely deprived or sincerely mixed-up in what should be a purer form of cultural life.

That the Japanese Americans of Hawaii are not totally accepted as Japanese or as Americans is most readily evident when they leave Hawaii and visit Japan or the mainland United States. For example, when Japanese Americans visit Japan, the land of their cultural heritage, the Japanese look upon them as strangers, as anomalies with Oriental faces and Occidental tongues. While in Japan, the Sansei especially appear awkward or out of place. The American influences on personality and appearance render the way they walk, talk, dress, eat and behave peculiar to Japanese who are not accustomed to the brashness of American youth. The Japanese look at the Sansei and ask, "What are you? Eskimo? Indian? Mexican?" When the startled Sansei proudly replies that he is of Japanese ancestry, the disbelieving Japanese shake their heads. "No, no. It is not possible! You are too dark to be Japanese!"

As if their unusally deep tans weren't complications enough, most Japanese Americans in Japan suffer from a serious language difficulty due to their inability to speak proper Japanese. In Hawaii, the typical Japanese American Sansei or Yonsei learns Japanese either from his early training in language schools or from the words and phrases which are used frequently in Hawaii's community. They soon learn that in Japan a vocabulary limited to *benjō,* bathroom or *bakatare,* fool, plus a few other phrases is not sufficient to impress Japanese with whom they try to converse.

Even the older Isseis, speaking the Japanese of their youth from the Meiji Era of late nineteenth century Japan, mixed with a smattering of pidgin English, have a language problem in Japan. An elderly Issei grandmother from Hawaii, who fulfilled her dream of returning to Japan before she died, was staying with her relatives on a farm near Hiroshima. One day, after she had prepared lunch for the men working in the fields she went out to call them in to eat. She shouted, "Oi, ooru men come kau kau, pau hana hana." Of course, the men found her words gibberish and continued on with their work.

By the same token when a Japanese American from Hawaii travels to many parts of the mainland he is at first thought to be a foreign visitor and is expected to have a passport, eat nothing but bowls of rice and sell transistor radios. Indeed when a man of the stature of Senator Daniel Inouye can so thoughtlessly be called a "little Jap" at the time of the Watergate hearings, it is done with the ignorance and bias that these Asians of Japanese ancestry, who call themselves Americans, are at best tourists from strange lands rather than fellow citizens.

The Japanese Americans from Hawaii also must face the realization that on the mainland the "English" they speak, in many cases, is not the English which mainland Americans can always understand. Even if they don't use a strong pidgin, they will use phrases, intonations and gestures which remain unintelligible to "standard" Americans.

In addition, when it is known that he is from the Islands, the Japanese American must confront the stereotypes which Americans project on Hawaii. "Do you hula? Do you eat poi? Do you like living in a grass

shack? Do you ever get rock bound?'' they ask innocently. But what becomes obvious to the Japanese
American is that he encounters the same kind of identity problem as he would in Japan. In neither the United
States nor Japan is the Japanese American of Hawaii
seen as an integral part of the cultural community. In
both cases he is seen as an oddity, as someone who
doesn't exactly fit in.

This problem occurs in America not necessarily because of the cliché reasons of white racism but because
the Japanese American of Hawaii remains an unknown
entity nationally. Including the Japanese Americans on
the mainland, the total number of Japanese Americans
who live in the United States amounts to only .291 percent of the total population. Japanese Americans do
not even constitute 1 percent of the American public;
they don't even make up three-tenths of 1 percent. Considering the fact that most Americans know even less
about the Island State, it stands to reason that Americans in general know relatively nothing about the Japanese Americans of Hawaii and would tend to view them
as outside of the mainstream of American life.

But to the Japanese American who lives in Hawaii,
standing outside of the mainstream of America and
Japan ''ain't no big thing.'' Instead of having an identity crisis which most ethnic groups are alleged to suffer
as a result of American acculturation, they recognize
their self-satisfaction that they are neither Americans of
America nor Japanese of Japan—they are simply Japanese Americans of Hawaii. The culture and lifestyle
they possess are gratifying and compatible with the Island environment in which they live, work, save, play,
laugh, cry and love.

In fact, these Island people have little desire or intention to identify with Japan Japanese or America Americans. They are quite content with being themselves and even find the Japanese and Americans in many cases to be peculiar and culturally different. For example, when some Sansei males talk about Japanese tourist girls, they say that their beauty is hard to appreciate. "Girls from Japan have weird faces," they complain. "They wear too much lipstick and are too pale. And their bodies are pear-shaped, flat on top and dumpy on the bottom. Their legs are ugly, cucumber-shaped. You know, *daikon* legs!"

The Sansei girls are not without their comments about Japanese tourist males. "Those Japanese guys," one Japanese American girl said, "walk, talk, eat and dress funny. They're typical FOBs, Fresh Off the Boats, or *Bobura,* pumpkin heads. The old men, too, act strange. They all wear money belts, walk around with their zippers down or use their underwear for swimming suits. Some are so stupid, they wash themselves outside the bathtub Japanese style, flooding the hotel floors."

As in the case of the Japanese tourist, when the Japanese American in Hawaii views the haole or white American from the mainland, he does so with a bit of aloofness; he tries to keep his cultural and psychological distance. In spite of the widely circulated notion which interprets an ethnic group's identity as striving to be "white," hardly admirable is the Island image of the "dumb haole," quick with the mouth, rattling foolishness, arrogant and cocky. The haole is not so much a symbol to be emulated as he is a characterized set of behaviors to be avoided. It is common to hear the admonition "No act like one haole!" And there is a sting of resentment at being accused of being too "haolefied."

This is not to say that on other levels, in certain circumstances, the haole and the Japanese American do not have a good relationship—in many ways they do. But the notion that the current day Japanese American strives to be similar to and accepted by the haole is as inaccurate as the assumption that Japanese Americans strive to pattern themselves after the Japanese tourist. If haoles of America and Japanese of Japan do not look at the Japanese American as complete brethren, neither does the Japanese American view them as people from whom he must demand love and acceptance.

Stated simply, there are underlying differences among the cultures of the haole, Japanese American and Japanese which means that no group totally identifies with or wants to identify with the other groups. While the Japanese American of Hawaii shares many of the same cultural features of both Japan and America he has, over the course of one hundred years of Island living, developed an identity separate from either of the monoliths of the Pacific.

And it should be noted that the Japanese American of Hawaii also feels to some degree separate from his Japanese American counterpart on the mainland, the Kotonk. The origin of the word Kotonk is still a very vague issue, but the theories on its origins set the tone for the relationship between the mainlander and the Island Japanese American. Some contend that the word originates from the sound of a falling coconut hitting the head of a Japanese American from the mainland. Others say that the word originates from World War II experiences of Japanese Americans in the army. When Japanese American inductees from Hawaii and the mainland were recruited into the 442 Nisei Combat Team, they got to know each other for the first time.

Naturally there were many ill feelings as the two groups tried to adapt to each other's ways of life and consequently an occasional fight would break out. During one such fight, the story goes, a Hawaiian recruit knocked a mainlander to the floor. When the mainland Japanese American's head hit the floor it went "Kotonk." From then on, supposedly, the word Kotonk was applied by Hawaii's Japanese Americans to any Japanese American from the mainland.

But the real conflict between the Kotonk and the Islander comes as a result not of the name calling but cultural variation. The most obvious cultural differences are exposed in the language of the two groups. As one Japanese American of Hawaii observed of Kotonks, "They think they speak so much better than locals. They think they speak good Standard American English. They think they have good pronunciation, enunciation and articulation. The Kotonks also think they have such a distinguished haole vocabulary." For example, the stereotype goes that if a Hawaii Japanese American talked about having a good time, he would say, "terrific, yeah," whereas the Kotonk would say, "yes, it was marvelous."

The stereotype of the Kotonk then, is that he is too haolefied; he tries to act better than Hawaii's Japanese Americans; he thinks he's too sophisticated and is therefore arrogant. As one rather vocal, local Japanese American grumbled, "Ooh, those Kotonks, they're as bad as those Japanese going to Punahou. I jus' can't stand 'em!"

When he is in Hawaii, the Kotonk has a difficult time readjusting his lifestyle so as to harmonize with the Island Japanese Americans. At a restaurant after everyone has eaten and the bill comes, local Japanese argue,

"I'll pay!" "No, I'll pay." "No, I'll pay." But the stereotypes locals have of Kotonks show them to be much different: "Here, you pay." "No, you pay." "No, I paid last time!" And even the more simple aspects of life in Hawaii supposedly cannot be adapted by Kotonks. One Kotonk confided that when he first learned that people in Hawaii actually ate spam and vienna sausage as a staple, and liked them, he couldn't believe it. On the mainland spam and vienna sausage certainly aren't served on a breakfast menu at any restaurant; they are mostly used as last resorts on camping or fishing trips or in case of extreme poverty. And never is that kind of food to be enjoyed!

If we recognize that the cultural world of the Japanese Americans in Hawaii differs from that of the Japanese of Japan, the Americans of America or the Japanese Americans of the mainland, then we must ask, "Who is the Japanese American of Hawaii? What are the cultural lifestyles by which he and his children live? Why is it that he has developed a way of life so different from that of his Japanese American brother on the mainland?"

But before these questions can be answered, we must seriously analyze the reasons behind a book of this nature. Why study the Japanese Americans of Hawaii instead of the Japanese of California, New York or Illinois? What can we hope to learn from an understanding of their culture and way of life which can have meaning for other peoples?

First, unlike Japanese Americans on the mainland and most other ethnic groups, the Hawaii population of Japanese Americans constitutes an ethnic group which is not a typical minority culture. Instead of representing a miniscule portion of the Island populace, the Japanese Americans of Hawaii until very recently were the largest ethnic group. Though now displaced from that position by the haole population, they still are a significant part of the community. Recent statistics indicate that over 200,000 Japanese Americans live in the State of Hawaii, about 28 percent of the total population. On the islands of Hawaii, Kauai, and Maui, they are the largest single ethnic group.

So when we talk about the Japanese Americans of Hawaii, we are not talking about the common cloistered group of ethnic minorities attempting to stay afloat in a sea of non-Japanese faces. Rather, we are talking about a group which not only sustains itself economically and psychologically, but a group which makes major contributions to the community of Hawaii as a whole.

Another reason why the Japanese American of Hawaii merits attention is that in comparison to many other states on the mainland, the population in Hawaii is truly a symbol of a mixture of cultures. Situated on a chain of volcanic islands mid-way between the great cultural centers of Japan and the United States, the Japanese American has adapted a number of different cultural inputs into his way of life. He has been able to incorporate and preserve some of the traditions, patterns and customs of Japan and America while at the same time assimilating enough Island culture so as to be able to cooperate with other local groups on an equal footing. In this way he has developed a "mindset," a world-view which to the humanist, anthropologist, sociologist, psychologist or layman is an intriguing source of data on human cultural interaction.

There is also another reason why I feel the identity of the Japanese American of Hawaii demands examination. After living in Hawaii a number of years and after having come into contact with all ethnic groups, one becomes aware that, without sounding too Walt Disneyish, Hawaii must certainly come close to being the "Magic Isles." Not that the Islands are a total Paradise; social ills and evils persist. Not that the people are all angelic or good-willed; human variance from greed to mundaneness to genius is a fact of life. Not that the ethnic groups mingle freely and openly at all times; prejudice, cultural and racial misunderstandings can still be found in one form or another.

But the Islands and its people are "magical" because they are strangely alluring. Patterns of life established in the urban settings of the mainland, including detachment and suspicion, become difficult to maintain among people whose openness and friendly manners are not all that far from their rural cultural roots. Indeed those involved in studying the Japanese Americans in Hawaii and their "identity" will eventually do so not because they will necessarily uncover any revealing and earth-shattering truths but simply because they will grow to like the people of Hawaii.

Yet, let me state unequivocally that while this book concerns itself with Japanese American identity, it will not tell you what a Japanese American *is*. If I said that a "Japanese American is *this*," then someone could effectively argue that, "No, they are *that*." After all, we are not talking about 200,000 Japanese Americans who are the same or without individuality. They are not a unidimensional, stereotypic group; human variations in life, values, experiences and insights are as real in the Japanese American community in Hawaii as in any other group of people. Therefore, in this book I will not be so presumptuous as to define the Japanese American identity of Hawaii but rather will explore some of the many factors which have gone into shaping that identity.

It is my belief that if you want to know what Japanese Americans are, first look at their families. Look at the system of sibling and parental interactions and the mechanisms of shame and filial piety. If you want to know whom they love or what values they place on their self-identity, look at their attitudes of sexuality and ideals of beauty which operate in the Island community.

If you want to know with whom Japanese Americans have fun and by whom they are influenced, look to their friends and peer group. Understand the forms of obligation and close associations which have their origins in cultural systems alien to the individualism of Western society. Look, also, to their community values of group support.

To comprehend why the Japanese Americans of Hawaii are different from their Japanese American mainland counterparts, look to the past to sense the relationship between ethnic peoples in Hawaii. The Japanese Americans do not exist in a condition of isolation; they do not constitute a people who live in an ethnic ghetto. The identity they possess is not formed solely within the confines of the ethnic group but as a result of the interrelationship of cultures in Hawaii. So if you want to perceive the historical antecedents of that intergroup identity look to the legacy of friendship and mutual understanding between Japan and Hawaii which determined to a large measure the compatibility of their people. If you want to comprehend the uneasiness, the deference or the hostility between ethnic groups, look to the legacy of prejudice and second-class citizenship which to some degree has characterized the Japanese Americans' past.

In addition, no interpretation can end without an analysis of the current status of the intergroup relations in Hawaii. The sharing of cultures in Hawaii, especially as it exists on a personal, day-to-day level, must be looked at to perceive why many Japanese Americans identify primarily with living in Hawaii and only secondarily with being Japanese or American.

The chapters of this book will cover these areas so that the reader can become sensitive to some of the various dimensions of the Japanese American identity. This book is not intended to be totally comprehensive; it is not a history of the Japanese American people in Hawaii, a complete analysis of their culture or a sociological description of their current status. Instead, the intention has been to study an ethnic group living in Hawaii from various perspectives so as to emerge with a clearer understanding of what it means to be a Japanese American. As a result, this book represents an attempt to survey unexplored ground when compared with other works which have tried to describe the Japanese American identity. For example, some studies have said that "You must understand acculturation to understand the Japanese Americans. The Americanization process is the key to their minds and lifestyles." Such books have gone on to examine the cultural features of Japan and America with only an occasional reference to the Japanese American culture itself.

Others have said of the Japanese American experience that "it is the history of an ethnic group under economic and racial exploitation. The struggle of a people against the might of a capitalistic system and the colonization of their souls to American consumerism best describe the Japanese situation." These studies have gone on to explore the ramifications of racism in South

Africa and the socialist systems of China, again with only passing mention of the Japanese American of Hawaii.

Finally, there are those who say that "the Japanese Americans must be examined from the viewpoint of Japan. At heart, they are still Japanese." Those books go on to discuss Japanese painting, dancing and music as if these were the most important factors in the life of Japanese Americans. Many times such studies are printed in Japanese as if all Japanese Americans could understand the language.

This book recognizes the importance of the Japanese cultural antecedents, the history of exploitation and the process of Americanization but will not dwell on them. The Japanese American of Hawaii deserves more merit than to be measured against the aged and warped yardstick of "Is he Japanese or is he American?" He is neither, nor does he necessarily want to be identified with either. "Is he racially exploited or is he a social equal?" is another worn question which increasingly has little relevancy to the situation of Japanese Americans in Hawaii; the Japanese American considers himself to be an integral part of the Hawaiian Islands with freedom of action and thought. Indeed the most relevant question which can be asked is "How is it that all of Hawaii's people have been able to live so compatibly and with such a profound sharing of cultures?"

This question is essential because when the tourist from Japan or Iowa observes the Japanese American interacting with friends and relatives at a Sunday Ken picnic in Ala Moana Park, he is seeing more than 100 people eating or playing games; he is watching, to some extent, the world of a people who have come to incorporate in their way of life a remarkable blending of cultures. From shave ice, to *"Tsuki ga deta deta,"* to *ope-lu,* to Kentucky Fried Chicken, to "Easy, brah," the Japanese American finds himself in the midst of a cultural synthesis whose ramifications have yet to be understood or realized.

Thus in the following pages we will see how the Japanese American interacts with his family, his friends, and other ethnic groups in Hawaii because these are the criteria with which he measures himself and from which his unique identity has been developed. From witnessing the dynamic interplay of cultures, family and friends taking place in the Hawaiian environment, perhaps we can all better grasp what is meant when a local says he "acts like one Japanee."

2
How Shame Fo' Da Family

Kiyoshi and Keiko Kitagawa live a quiet life. Kiyoshi wears his gray hair in a close-shaved crew cut and he favors white shirts and gray baggy trousers. Keiko also likes the color gray in her clothing. She wears no make-up but she is always neat and clean; her hair is always pulled back into a tight bun. On some days the elderly Issei couple go shopping together, catching the bus in a crowd of other Isseis, showing their over-65 free pass and carrying their brown paper shopping bags by the handle. Their favorite television station is Channel 13 and their favorite program is *Dai Chūshingura*. They know all the names of the sumo wrestlers, and they like Japanese movies but sometimes think there is too much sex.

Kiyoshi's earliest memories of Japan are of the time he was seven years old and going to school. Besides his regular lessons of reading, writing and learning arithmetic, he was taught to sit straight, to honor and love his homeland, to sacrifice his life for Japan. He learned the values of *shūshin,* moral training, which engrained in his young mind the devotion to his family and ancestors.

Gakkō wa kibishikatta, school was strict, is the impression Kiyoshi has of both his schooling and upbringing in Japan. The province of Atachi in Fukushima, where Kiyoshi was born in 1889, was a rural district inhabited by farmers who eked a living off the land. After Kiyoshi finished the eighth grade, he worked on his father's farm until he was 18 years old. Then he made a momentous decision which would change the course of his life.

Perhaps he had talked to a friend, who talked to a friend who knew someone who had labored in Hawaii and had returned to Japan wealthy. By chance he might have read a small booklet entitled "The New Hawaii" which was circulating in Japan at that time and which created a romantic and attractive picture of plantation work in Hawaii. Perhaps he was disenchanted with the future prospects of being a farmer in Japan, the poor quality of the land and a crop of *kome,* rice, which Kiyoshi remembers as being "junk." Or perhaps Kiyoshi was simply a youthful adventurer who saw life in Hawaii as an alluring and exciting change from the life of a Japanese farmer.

For whatever reason, at the age of 18 and against the wishes of his parents, Kiyoshi boarded a steamer which would take him and some 250 other Japanese males to "the land of bountiful plenty," the Hawaiian Islands. Before he left, his parents presented him with a gift of a sewing box which they could ill-afford. But without a mother or wife to care for him, they realized that for Kiyoshi to look proper and well-kept he would need to mend his clothing with a sufficient supply of needle and thread.

After ten days of a crowded and rough ocean voyage, the 250 immigrant laborers from Japan, including Kiyoshi Kitagawa, arrived at the port of Honolulu and were processed through the immigration station at Sand Island. Hearing that work was to be found on Ewa Plantation, Kiyoshi went there only to find too many men looking for jobs. So the following day he took the boat to Kauai where he found work on the McBryde Plantation as a field laborer.

The dreams of adventure and wealth that Kiyoshi had before coming to work in Hawaii were soon dissolved by the more demanding realities of plantation life. Working in the rows of sugar cane, cutting, loading and hauling ten hours a day, six days a week, Kiyoshi earned 69ᶜ a day, $18 a month. Kiyoshi remembers that his *luna* was Portuguese and a fair man. But the conditions in which he lived were squalid. The men were crowded into a small room and their personal area consisted of the amount of space required to sleep. The toilets he remembers were *pilau* and *kitanai,* stinky and dirty.

Kiyoshi had never intended to make Hawaii his home. He had hopes of returning to Japan when he had had his fill of adventure and had earned enough money to live a life of wealth in his village in Fukushima. But as he grew older and his wealth never materialized, he realized that his hopes of returning to Japan were unrealistic. It appeared to Kiyoshi that Hawaii was to be his home. Being lonely, it also appeared that now was the time for female companionship. So Kiyoshi decided that he would write to his parents in Japan and ask them to select from his village a proper Japanese woman to be his wife. He went to a photographer who for a small price would take Kiyoshi's picture; he even provided Kiyoshi with a cleanly pressed suit. Other Japanese bachelors also visited the photographer to obtain self-portraits to send to prospective brides in Japan. There were even some laborers, a little too old or worn from the plantation work, who would have a handsomer or more youthful friend pose for them. But not Kiyoshi. He wanted his future bride to know exactly what he looked like before she came to Hawaii.

Keiko Koizumi was 16 years old and an attractive young lady. She too was born in the same village as Kiyoshi in Fukushima prefecture. Of her youth in Japan, Keiko remembers swimming in the cold rivers, picking fruit in the dense woods of the mountains and teasing wild monkeys she and her friends would find there. Keiko left school after the fourth grade because she did not like it. After all, the course of her life would be to learn the trades and duties of a woman and a future wife, not a scholar. She was quite content with her life in Japan and had no thought of ever up-rooting herself by leaving.

But one day she was approached by her parents who had brought her some pictures to see. Though Keiko didn't understand what was going on, she did as her parents told her and selected the picture of the man she most preferred. Two weeks later she found out that she was going to an island called Hawaii to marry a man named Kiyoshi Kitagawa. In her heart she was fearful and confused; she didn't want to leave her family, friends and country to live with a man she didn't know. But as the eldest child she was obligated to fulfill her duty to her parents. Her family was poor and the money which Keiko could send from the rich land of Hawaii, *Tenjiku* or Heavenly Place, would help immensely.

In 1916, accompanied by her younger brother Hiroshi, Keiko took a steamer to Honolulu. It was the first time she had ever left her village and she cried and cried. On board ship there were about 125 other women who were also picture brides. The voyage took nine days and Keiko was seasick during the entire trip. When they arrived in Honolulu and were inspected at the immigration station, Keiko's "heart was thumping with fear," *mune ga doki doki shimashita*. The immigration officials asked for a sample of her feces to inspect for possible diseases but Keiko was too nervous to cooperate. She was so scared being in a foreign land, she couldn't move her bowels; Hiroshi had to give her half of his.

As she left the immigration station, she saw a crowd of Japanese men waiting, pictures in hand, looking for their brides. The women, too, held small photos in their hands looking for their handsome husbands, who occasionally turned out to be 30 years older or less attractive than their counterfeit photos indicated. But Keiko and Kiyoshi recognized each other immediately, and each approached the other and hesitantly bowed.

According to Japanese custom, Kiyoshi and Keiko were already legally married. But United States officials insisted on an American ceremony for all picture brides which was performed for the 125 couples at the immigration station *en masse*. After this ritual, the couple took the boat to Kauai where they lived in a village comprised mostly of other Japanese. The small Japanese community made young Keiko feel comfortable since it wasn't too different from her village in Japan.

As a Japanese wife it was Keiko's obligation to keep her husband happy even though she had to make personal sacrifices. Every morning she would wake up before Kiyoshi when it was still dark to make him a hot breakfast. His working clothes had to be kept clean and

As the women left the immigration station, there was a crowd of Japanese men waiting, pictures in hand, looking for their brides. *Actual picture bride photograph courtesy of the Kaji-ura Collection.*

his *bentō*, lunch, had to be prepared. By the time he came home from the fields, Keiko had Kiyoshi's dinner waiting as well as a hot bath and clean clothes. At night Keiko did not go to bed until Kiyoshi was in bed first. And whenever he wanted to make love, she was never "too tired" or "sick" but always cooperated. In addition to all these chores, Keiko also worked in the planta-tion fields alongside her husband.

"Today our life is good," they reflect. But they re-member those early years of *hoe hana, hana wai* and *ha-pai ko;* weeding, irrigating and harvesting, with mixed feelings. They were years of toil and hardship but dur-ing that time Keiko happily gave birth to five children—three boys, Masa, Asao and Shigeru, and two girls, Harumi and Yukiko.

Masa was the eldest son of Kiyoshi and Keiko, born in 1917 on the island of Kauai. In 1927, his father who had saved his hard-earned money so that his first son could have a good education, sent Masa to Honolulu. Boarding at the Reverend Takie Okumura's home, Masa learned to read and write Japanese, as well as to recite the tenets of Christianity. When he was of age, he entered McKinley High School which he attended every morning by walking from the Okumura home on South King Street.

Growing up in the Hawaii of the 1920s and 1930s was not eventful for Masa. The years were characterized by odd jobs such as newspaper boy, store clerk for the local Japanese grocery market or tray boy at Hawaiian Pineapple Co. Since he was a competent student, his sights were set on attending the University of Hawaii. Consequently, he always saved his money.

During the summer months he returned to Kauai to be with his family and work for the McBryde Planta-

The years of *hoe hana* are remembered with mixed feelings. They were years of hardship for the Issei, but they were also the years in which the young immigrant couples began to raise their families. *Photo courtesy of the Fukuda Collection.*

tion. At home, Masa didn't have any of the problems communicating with his parents that younger Nisei were having since he was taught to speak, read and write Japanese. On the other hand, he spoke enough English to be considered quite proficient in the language. But he never lost, nor wanted to lose, his ability to speak in Island dialect, pidgin.

When Masa was 20, he married 18-year-old Evelyn Yamamoto, a girl approved by his parents from his village on Kauai. The wedding was performed at a Christian church; the bride wore an American-style wedding gown and was given a ring. But at the reception, the bride wore a kimono and the couple was toasted *banzai* in the traditional Japanese manner.

Now married and wanting children, Masa began to work full time. Giving up his notions of going on to the University, he was working as a clerk at the Bank of Hawaii when war broke out between Japan and America in 1941.

When America and Hawaii were preparing for a war in Europe and the Pacific, Masa already had one child, a two-year-old daughter named Carol, and another on the way. The question of to which country a Japanese American felt loyal was never an issue for Masa. At heart he belonged in Hawaii, not Japan. If his homeland of Hawaii came under attack he would defend it. That he was an American, that he felt an emotional bond with the country of his citizenship, he never doubted.

When the Japanese Americans of Hawaii were offered a chance to volunteer for an all-Nisei combat team, Masa and one of his close friends had a serious and heated argument. Masa felt that as Americans who lived in Hawaii, Japanese Americans had a duty to defend the country of their birth. Anyway, with every eye on the Japanese American community, the young Nisei had to prove the loyalty and worth of their people. "Ridiculous," his friend argued. "We don't need to proved anything. You know, Hawaii isn't even a real part of the United States. This isn't my war and I'm not going to fight it."

The next day Masa went with his brothers, Asao and Shigeru, to the draft board to enlist. But during the medical examination it was found that Masa had a physical ailment and he was rejected for military service. Both of his brothers passed the physicals and were inducted into the army.

For the Masa Kitagawa family the war years were hard working years but they were also prosperous years. With military personnel and equipment flowing through Hawaii, the economy of the Islands was booming and everyone was benefiting from the new jobs which were available. But in January 1945 came the shocking and saddening news that Masa's brother Asao had been killed in Europe while defending his country in war.

After victory in Europe and Japan, Honolulu returned to being a peaceful community. Masa went to work for the Territory of Hawaii as an assistant supervisor in the Highway Department. He moved to a new home in Kaimuki which he purchased so that he and his wife could raise their three children, Carol, Ed and Frank, in a secure and friendly neighborhood.

Masa's daughter, Carol, grew up in urban Honolulu and is a third generation Sansei Japanese American elementary school teacher with the Department of Education. She is married to another Sansei, David En-do, who was born and raised on Maui. They had met at the University of Hawaii where he was working towards his degree in Business Administration and she towards her teaching credential. Now a Certified Public Accountant, he and Carol are bringing up their two children in their new Pearl City home.

The way they are raising their children is not so different from the way that Carol was raised. Going to public school with children of all racial backgrounds, though hanging out predominantly with Japanese, in the afternoon Carol's children attend Japanese language school. The parents expect their children to finish public school and then go on to college, though what they will eventually become is left up to them.

Carol and David are grateful that their children are growing up in Hawaii; it's a good place to live and learn. And they are also grateful that their children are fortunate enough to have great-grandparents which they as Sansei never had. For them, the appreciation of the love within the family is enhanced when children can participate in many of the joyous gatherings which bring together the rich heritage of the family members.

After their many years raising and watching the family grow from one generation to another, Keiko and Kiyoshi Kitagawa are now observing their fifty-fifth wedding anniversary at the home of their son Masa, where the elderly Issei couple now live. Besides Keiko and Kiyoshi, their children and their children's children have gathered. Carol and her husband have brought their two sons who are outside playing with their cousins.

Inside the small Kaimuki home the women are preparing a large meal of *teriyaki, sashimi, sushi, tempura,* roast turkey, macaroni salad, *nishime,* sweet and sour spareribs, *ogo-namasu* and, of course, rice. If the women are not fixing the meal they are preparing the serving table or washing the dirty dishes. Keiko and Kiyoshi speak very little English, mostly Japanese with some Hawaiian and pidgin words thrown in. They sit on the couch, listening, watching, and frequently giving a brief but radiant smile as if they understand the conversation or remember something pleasant from the past.

All the males sit in the parlor, drinking beer, eating from their paper plates with their *hashi,* chopsticks, "talking story" and laughing. Occasionally their wives will join them, but more often the women are tending the kitchen or watching the children.

Under this roof in Kaimuki are four generations of Japanese Americans who have created a home in Hawaii. Each generation, with its own special insights, has participated in the forces and events which form our Island heritage. The Kitagawas, celebrating a gathering of the generations, are a Japanese American family. They are but one of countless families who have shared a similar past and find a similar quality in their styles of living.

The Kitagawas, from Kiyoshi to Masa to Carol are fictional characters. They do not exist but the drama and patterns of their lives have existed for four generations of Japanese Americans. Of course the Japanese Americans of Hawaii cannot be portrayed from a single family perspective. The dimensions of their experiences and lifestyles are too varied and multiple to be categorized from such a single standpoint. For everyone who says the experience was oppressive and harrowing, there will be others to testify that it was fulfilling and pleasant. For those who found Hawaii to be a Hell, there are those who found it to be a Heaven. And there are a great many Japanese who have thought of the Hawaiian Islands as simply being a good home.

Despite the diversity of experiences and attitudes found among Japanese Americans, there is one common denominator, however, which is illustrated in the story of the Kitagawas. In practically all circumstances, the Japanese American identifies primarily with his family. The grandparents, the parents, the children, the uncles, aunties and cousins form the nucleus of the historical, cultural, sociological and psychological referents with which a Japanese American structures his life.

It is within the family that the child is weaned and nurtured; he is given the values, directions and motivations necessary to perpetuate the community in which he lives. The moral and personal standards which define the "good life" are taught to him through his family, as are the emotional bonds to his cultural group. It is more than fitting, therefore, to begin to look at the Japanese American identity by looking at the Japanese American family of Hawaii.

Doing so, you should keep in mind that the family is not just the mother, father and child. The family is an organism of extended relationships which spans the generations of immigration, plantation labor, war hysteria, Americanization and day-to-day living. Within the family can be found not only a history of a people, but an understanding of the cultural lifestyles which they have developed and lived.

For an outsider to understand the Japanese American family, and for an insider to stay in it, two important factors must be considered. First, it must be remembered that although it might appear that the Japanese

The Japanese American family of Hawaii—three generations. *Photo courtesy of the Sato Collection.*

American family is a nuclear-type family with parent and sibling, it is in fact an extended one. Very few Japanese American families in Hawaii are isolated from the close, daily contact with an extensive potpourri of relatives. My guess would be that during an average day, a housewife will be on the phone with at least two different relatives outside of the home.

The other aspect of the Japanese American family which commands prime importance is what could be called the Family Image. Now most Japanese Americans in Hawaii know what I am talking about when I say that "one must maintain the Family Image." They know that living in the Japanese American family is like living in a glass house. Whether their home is Kahului, Kapaa, Hilo, Honolulu or Waipahu, they know that their neighbors, relatives and friends know everything that goes on in their family and will gossip, given the chance. Stories circulate among the Issei, Nisei and Sansei about who has to get married because she's pregnant, who's getting a divorce because of an illicit affair, which family has a son smoking marijuana, or a daughter taking the Pill.

Needless to say, under such circumstances there is a high degree of family comparisons being made— "Which Family Image is the purest, most respectable?" Parents lecture to their children that whatever they do, "Don't forget what you could do to our Family Image!" Son and daughter must constantly work at being "good," being "successful," being "well-behaved." The children are reminded that "The Yamamura's boy isn't like you. Can't you be like him, so smart and well-behaved?"

You can imagine that for children, such constant comparisons can be both frustrating and confusing.

One local Japanese American told me that in his family he was always being told by his parents that they wished he would be as "good" as his friend Mitsuo. "Can't you be like Mitsuo?" his mother would lament anytime he did anything wrong. Well one time, he went to his mother and asked if he could have a new motorcycle. When she said no, he pleaded with her that all his friends were getting them, including Mitsuo. His mother carried on, "Can't you ever listen to your own conscience? Do you have to do everything your no good friends do? Why do you have to be like them?"

At any rate, the Japanese American parent, and this is cross-generational, has a platonic ideal of the perfect boy and girl. Such children must never talk back to their parents or disobey a parental order. They must never dress or act like hippies with excessively long hair, loose morals or drug usage. In addition, for the girls especially, they must never smoke or drink alcohol.

Above all, to preserve the Family Image, to avoid nasty rumors and prevent snide comparisons, it is absolutely necessary that both son and daughter date and eventually marry a good Japanese American. For them to do otherwise is asking for trouble and even disownment.

For example, I knew a Japanese American girl who fell in love with a Korean. When the two decided that they wanted to get married, her parents told her bluntly, "You listen and you listen good. If you marry that Korean we will not only lose a daughter but you will lose a family."

In this case, love was stronger than parental obligation and the girl disobeyed her parents and married her Korean fiancé. Her parents never condoned the marriage, refused to go to the wedding and didn't speak to their daughter for two years. Only after the girl gave birth to a son making her parents grandparents did they accept their daughter and son-in-law back into the family. But even then, whenever the parents would talk about their daughter's husband they would apologize, "Well, my son-in-law is Korean. But you know, he is really Japanese in his ways!"

Part of the Family Image which has to be maintained is the illusion of "overachievement." A Japanese American family cannot be average, run-of-the-mill or mundane. The family members must be the best at whatever they attempt; their Image must be unblemished and exemplary.

The "overachievement" which is the motivation behind the Japanese American family seems to have its results. Keeping up with and outdistancing the Watanabes have resulted in the creation of a community which has been referred to as "model," "most successful" and "truly the best" of any in the United States. Statistically, Japanese American families have the lowest divorce rate, lowest crime rate, lowest juvenile delinquency rate, lowest illegitimate birth rate and highest indices of educational achievement.

Viewing these achievements, you could hypothesize that being part of a Japanese American family would either be a joy of self-respect or a burden of boredom. Speaking as a member of a Japanese American family, let me say that the family is at once a joy and a burden. While statistics reveal the surface accomplishments of creating and perpetuating a solid Family Image, they do not speak to some of the pressures put upon each family member. A few students tell me that the only reason they are in school, doing poorly I must admit, is because their parents give little choice. "Go to school, or get out of this family." Older Nisei family men, despite their urges and curiosity, refuse to go to clubs or pornography movies on Hotel Street for fear of being recognized by someone. Mothers resist the desires to smoke or drink liquor because their husbands would not approve. Daughters turn down dates with boys they like because the boys have a "bad reputation" or are not Japanese.

To maintain the Family Image, then, is an important end of familial relations. All the members of the Japanese American family are subject to the mechanisms of compliance to the standards of behavior which keep up their Image.

One of the mechanisms which has been developed by the parents to help the children conform to family needs is the technique of the "final wish." The "final wish" technique is especially effective on daughters who begin to act recalcitrant. As the daughter graduates from high school, she decides that she isn't interested in going to college and starts to look for a job as a secretary. Horrified, the parents plead with her to at least go to community college. "This is our final wish," they beg.

So she goes to community college and then to the University of Hawaii working diligently but not excessively, hoping to fulfill her parents' "final wish." When she at last graduates and wants to relax for a year and maybe go traveling, again her parents plead, "Please go on to get your teaching credentials. After this final wish then you may do as you like."

The daughter is obedient once again as she student teaches for a year and then gets a job with the Department of Education as a secondary school teacher. As you can expect, after this accomplishment she wants to get her own apartment and move away from home.

"Oh no," respond her parents. "It is our final wish that you live at home until you find a good Japanese boy to marry."

The "final wish" never ends. It remains a constant pressure which hangs over the children of a Japanese American family helping them to remember how to keep the Family Image healthy. But to understand the effectiveness of the "final wish" the value of filial piety for the Japanese American family must be appreciated. While one may have heard about the idea of unconditional love between parents and offspring, in the Japanese American family the relationship between parent and child is typified more by unconditional piety. The child is taught from the earliest ages to honor and respect parents and is obligated to please them.

To the Japanese American parent, the child's obligation is natural and proper. After all, who brought the little one into the world? To whom does he have to give his undying thanks and gratitude? Who took care of the child when he was a helpless infant, nursing, pampering, protecting and nurturing him so that he could be healthy and strong? Wasn't it the parents who made the sacrifices while the child was growing up? It was they who did without so that the child could have, have, have. Instead of eating out at restaurants, they saved their money so that their children could buy musical instruments for the school band. The mother never bought new clothes but sewed her own dresses so that the daughter could have money for new clothes bought at expensive, modish shops. Money was saved for the children's education and to pay for the increased automobile insurance for juvenile drivers.

With this frame of reference, it is easy to see why the parents feel that the children owe them something. The notion "you owe us" is the crux of filial piety; it is the basis upon which the child feels obligation to his parents.

Of course, not all children respond to filial piety with wholehearted enthusiasm. While certainly many of the things that a child feels obligated to do he will often enjoy doing, conflict can also occur. Instead of feeling thanks for being brought into the world, the little ingrate will look his parents straight in the eye and say, "Well, I never asked to be born. It's your fault that I came into the world. You have to pay for it, not me!"

After the shocked father has calmed down the mother who hysterically sobs, "My God, where did we go wrong?" the family fight ensues. I believe that in the Japanese American family arguments over the child's resistance to parental obligation and filial piety are the mainstay of topics in conflict. Anytime you see a Japanese American son and father or mother and daughter arguing, epithets of "You have to know your place," "I don't have to do things for you," "You must listen and respect what we say," or "I don't owe you anything," are sure to be hurled.

That an appeal to filial piety is often successful, though, in the maintenance of the Family Image can be seen in the case of the only daughter. Pampered, spoiled and put on a pedestal, the only girl is given much, and in return much is expected from her. As the only child in the family, she will inherit all the money and property which the parents have accumulated over the years. Because of their sacrifices and savings, the daughter will have a secure inheritance which their Issei parents could never give them. For this reason, the daughter must respond with devotion and obedience.

One can comprehend why, then, the parents are shattered when the only daughter becomes engaged to a man they consider to be "good for nothing." Both parents, especially the father, cannot bear the thought of all their money and life's work left in the hands of a beer-guzzling, long-haired heavy-equipment operator. The daughter owes them a lot more than the knowledge that their small estate will be spent on alcohol or rock music. Consequently, the daughter feels the compulsion to meet her parents' wishes by not marrying.

Despite the conflicts which might arise out of generational differences in perception of filial piety or how much or how little is obligated, the devotion and respect which a child shows to the parent in the Japanese American family remain perhaps the most powerful force to make children obey. Perhaps one can understand the low statistics of juvenile delinquency and illegitimate births, and the high statistics of educational achievement in the Japanese American community only from the perspective of filial piety. Rather than being innately "good" or having an "Oriental nature" without vices or illicit desires, one must look at the Japanese American child as constantly being checked and guided by parental inspection and decisions which the child feels a duty to obey.

In addition to the "final wish" and filial piety as mechanisms to enhance the Family Image and keep children "in line," there is the matter of "shame" which is used to help keep both parents and children in compliance with the ideal of the "good" family; "how shame fo' da family" is a very real control on the individual's behavior. Shame is based on the external sanctions of what others think and say about your actions. The concern is not what you think about yourself, but what your relatives, neighbors or community think about you. By your actions you can generate praise and respect which will build the Family Image, or criticism and contempt which will bring shame to you and your family.

This emphasis on avoiding shame should be differentiated from American middle class families where the primary form of social control is guilt. How you act according to your own conscience regardless of what others think, is the American way of maintaining good conduct. The horror of being guilty in your own eyes is what prevents you from stealing candy when no one is looking or cheating on your income tax returns. As Kipling poignantly wrote, "If YOU can keep your head when all about you/Are losing theirs . . . you'll be a Man, my son."

In the Japanese American community in Hawaii, Kipling would need liberal paraphrasing. "If you do something which others all around you won't approve of, you will be shamed, my son." Feeling shame isn't so much a feeling of doing what one feels is good for his conscience but what will reflect well on the family. Because you have brought shame to the Family Image, the guilt you feel is not for your actions but for the consequences they have created for your mother, your father, your grandparents and all your relatives.

While in an American context guilt is resolved through confession and absolution, shame is only multiplied when a guilt is confessed. More people will know your actions and therefore the shame will be greater. A Japanese American accused of a crime might plead guilty and actually be pardoned if his crime is a first offense. But in the Japanese American community, he will never be pardoned. His crime will cast a pall on his family who will be remembered as parents of a criminal. For many years to come the community will hold the offender and his family in low esteem.

In Hawaii the fear of shaming as a maintenance of Family Image can be interpreted as one reason why crime and divorce rates are so low in the Japanese American community. Instead of suffering the shame of committing a crime and getting caught or getting a divorce which lets everyone know how bad a husband or wife you are, it would be better to resist the temptations of crime and suffer a marriage of tedium or even hate. For the truth of the matter is, wherever you live, Maui, Kauai, Molokai, the Big Island or Oahu, people in your neighborhood will find it hard to forget what you do.

To cope with shame, the Japanese say that the traveler will leave shame behind. But in Hawaii where the average Japanese American stays in one place, in one neighborhood, it is unlikely that he will forego his emotional attachment to Hawaii, the quality of life in the Islands and chance the monetary uncertainties of moving a family to the mainland and finding new employment. Compared to the typical American middle class family which moves on an average six different times, the Japanese American of Hawaii is no traveler. His enduring personal ties to his neighbors and his commitment to live in Hawaii mean that the Japanese American must live with the realization of never causing shame to be cast upon his family by his actions.

The identity of a haole American has been characterized by the metaphor of a person walking a long street, lined with on-lookers. As the individual walks the street, an occasional on-looker glances at him, then turns away. He often proceeds without being watched.

The Japanese American is characterized as also walking a long street lined with on-lookers. But as he walks the street, every eye is on him. They watch his every movement, approving, disapproving. He is rarely given a moment of unwatched freedom. The Japanese American family is the primary on-looker that guides the lives of its respective members. And the community watches and guides the family so that an image is created which contributes to the ethnic group as a whole.

Viewed then as maintaining the Family Image, the "final wish," filial piety and shame are all key features of the Japanese American family. Any Issei, Nisei or Sansei knows how the mechanisms work, they know how to maximize their own desires while at the same time protecting their family. To an outsider such a system of family control might seem oppressive and personally destructive—to the insider it is known that often these devices can be used to one's advantage. The relationships between parents and siblings are, of course, not as restrictive as this discussion might have made them seem. There is much leeway and room for maneuvering so that children and parents not only work to maintain their Family Image, but satisfy their own needs and desires. While there are strict limits to what one can and cannot do in a Japanese American family, within these boundaries one can negotiate a wide range of actions.

There is an additional reason why the Japanese American family should not be construed as a singly oppressive entity, duplicated in the same patterns in every Japanese American home. Obviously such a sterotype is an impossibility based on the simple fact of human variation. As the Kitagawa family was shown to expand and develop during the Hawaiian experience, so too has the Japanese American family undergone serious modifications. One striking example of the changes still taking place in the family can be seen in the Yonsei and Gosei. Unlike the Nisei whose grandparents lived in Japan, and the Sansei whose grandparents spoke little English, the Yonsei will be the first Japanese American generation to have grandparents with whom they can communicate. While the basic focus of the Japanese American family has been parent to child, how will this change with the emergence of a grandparent relationship? Since grandparents are notorious for pampering and spoiling grandchildren, will the Yonsei and Gosei generations be seriously redefining and redesigning the mechanisms of control and Family Image which have characterized the Japanese American generations to date?

Thus, the Japanese American family must be viewed as an institution which involves many factors. Primarily the family is the transmitter of the ancestry and heritage of the Japanese American in Hawaii. The history, the traditions of the people are rooted in the family, and secondly the community. Through the family history one learns about his generation, his values and his identity in Hawaii.

The Japanese American family is also a way of life, a pattern of living which can be both a pleasure and a pain. Because of the goals of the family to attain a standard of the "good life," and gain the respect and admiration of others, more headaches and tensions have been created than might have seemed worthwhile at the time. But by so patiently persevering, the family has served itself, and its community, well.

3
Why Are You So Much Like Me?

Children often reveal through their games and rhymes
many of the foibles and exaggerated concerns with
which we as adults are so frequently preoccupied. By
taking matters to the extremes, their innocent sayings
and gibberish satirize the values and attitudes of the
society in which they so rapidly become enculturated.
The children of Hawaii as they create new games and
rhymes remain an excellent source for an understanding
of what is valued in the community. Indeed, if one takes
the time and effort to observe and listen to Island
youngsters, many insights into the cultural lifestyles of
adults can be discerned.

For example, it is possible to observe a small group of
children in Kaneohe, Honolulu or Hilo playing this simple game: One child chants "One, two, three, bumble-
bee, who's the lady with the big *chi-chis*?" On each
word the child points to each of the other children in a
manner not unlike "Eeny, Meeny, Miny, Mo?" The
child who is pointed to on the last word is the "lady
with the big *chi-chis*."

In a society steeped in a mammarian fetish, one which uses physical attractiveness as a primary focal point to judge a human being, this short rhyme raises an issue which has direct bearing on the nature of the Japanese American identity in Hawaii.

Besides the preservation of the Family Image, the concern with filial piety and shame, the Japanese American has a more than passing interest in sex. Sexual attraction, after all, is an important basis of marriage and the family. Without the attraction between males and females, the emotion of love and the cultural and psychological needs to spend one's life with another human being, there would be no husbands and wives to raise a family. Obviously, if the family and its continuity command importance in the Japanese American community then so also does sex.

And as revealed in the children's rhyme, what is important for most people including the Japanese American of Hawaii is sex as it is expressed in an ideal of beauty. For whether we like it or not, sex and love are predicated on physical attraction—the important question is all too often, "Who's the lady with the big *chichis*" or "Who's the man with the good build and dark complexion?"

Now maybe you met your girl friend or boy friend, husband or wife, on a Friday night at Zippy's Drive-In or on a blind date to Kapahulu Theater arranged through a friend. Or maybe you both grew up together attending the same public schools and college. At any rate, the first time you took a serious interest in your future mate, you looked at the face. Was it horribly repulsive or was it something worth showing off to your friends? Then you scanned the rest of the anatomy. Was the hair attractively arranged, trimmed and clean?

Was the body not seriously marred by midriff bulge or a crooked posture? Was there enough where it was needed and little where it wasn't? Could you rationalize in your mind that you would be proud to be seen with this person in a crowd, among friends or with your family?

One might argue that the sexual attraction between male and female is a very superficial basis for mate selection. After all, personality is important; no one can stand a braggart, a bore or a bum even if he or she is good looking. Isn't it important that you and your mate have a common interest, a mutual love for Rainbow basketball, *okazu* stands and *musubi*?

Yet it is almost a naive cliché to point out that the old adage "beauty is only skin-deep," is passé. To a frightening degree we still judge people more on their external physical appearance than on their personality or common interests. For example, how many people can honestly say that they treat an attractive person of the opposite sex the same way as someone who is unattractive? Does a flat-chested girl receive the same kind of attention as a buxom one? Does a six-foot replica of Burt Reynolds get the same kind of service as a five-foot replica of Woody Allen? Ideally we would hope the answers would be "yes." Realistically we must recognize that the nature of our sexually preoccupied society necessitates an answer of "no."

Cross-racially and ethnically, then, individuals come to share a common notion of what is or isn't sexually arousing; what is or isn't beautiful. Once this ideal of sexual beauty is developed and perpetuated, then the need to become beautiful and associate with beautiful people becomes paramount to many individuals as a means of self-evaluation and mate selection. To define this ideal of beauty as it operates in the community of Hawaii and as it is shared by the Japanese American is not an easy task. So many varied cultural inputs and attitudes have come together to create this ideal that the extraction of each element becomes difficult. However, the old argument that the standard of beauty for all Americans is the haole couple with blond hair and blue eyes is not totally accurate for Hawaii. Generally speaking we can talk about the creation of a concept of beauty and sexual attraction in the Islands which takes elements from the haole ideal of facial and body features and intermingles them with the image of the beautiful Oriental and Polynesian.

Probably the most striking example of this local image of beauty which has evolved as a consequence of the sharing of cultures is found in an advertisement in local newspapers for a clothing store geared to young people. The advertisement usually has a drawing of a young couple wearing some modish outfits promoting the store's clothing. The couple is of Oriental-Polynesian extraction, the girl in bikini and the male in a neat-fitting aloha shirt. The girl's hair is long and straight, her body petite and not buxom, her skin deeply tanned. She belongs not to the Orient but to Polynesian Hawaii where wearing bikinis and having dark tans is the norm. Also deeply tanned and giving off the image of a "beachboy," the male is not a tall and rugged man but physically well-proportioned and of normal stature. His hair is lengthy but neatly trimmed; his slanted-eyes are confident.

In many ways this local image of what is beautiful and sexually attractive appeals to the Sansei and other young people in Hawaii because it is a practical and feasibly attainable image. The local ideal of beauty is

A local image of what is beautiful. *Drawing by Masayo Suzuki.*

not a plastic, highly polished image removed from the level of reality. The couple who typify the young, beautiful people of Hawaii are not fantastic; their facial features are not unblemished or ideal. Most people with a little effort could create for themselves a sexual self-identity patterned on the local standard which would be comfortably anxiety-free.

That the local ideal of beauty is possibly attainable to the Japanese American in Hawaii is an essential concept which distinguishes the self-identity of the local Japanese American from the Kotonk or mainland Japanese American. In Hawaii the Japanese American is not made to feel overly conspicuous by his physical features. A short, Asian male can feel fairly comfortable walking among the hordes of shoppers at the Ala Moana Shopping Center because he is not alone. There are so many short Japanese American males like him that he doesn't have to feel physically inferior.

But on the mainland, the height of the Japanese male is one of the most conscious dissatisfactions. Within an environment which is largely haole, the ideal he has for the perfect, virile male is a six-foot three-inch Chad Everett or Rock Hudson. Being short and stocky, with a long torso and short legs in a world where beauty is measured in height, the Kotonk may feel more anxiety about his physical appearance than does the Japanese American of Hawaii.

In fact, some Japanese American males are perhaps even more conscious of their height than most people would expect. I can never forget a close friend of mine who confided to me that because he was so short, it was his obligation to his future children to marry a six-foot haole girl so that his genes could mix with hers and produce tall sons. On the mainland recently, a Japanese

American was trying to qualify as a policeman. Requirements demanded that policemen be a certain height but he was two inches too short. So for months, he had himself put into traction so as to stretch his body. Before he went for his physical examinations, he had his wife raise welts on his head by cracking him on his skull with a two-by-four board. Needless to say, with true Japanese determination, he would do anything to grow.

That the Kotonk recognizes the difference between what he is and the haole standard of beauty is not to say that the local Japanese American doesn't also feel some discrepancies. Although the local standard of beauty is much more conducive to the Japanese American psyche than a haole standard, frustrations can arise. People will still seek to alter themselves so as to fit the ideal more perfectly. For example, a local norm of beauty incorporates the haole style of round eyes and firm, well-proportioned breasts. Consequently many Japanese American females, attempting to be beautiful, use techniques and devices to round their slanting eyes and uplift their bust line. To correct the slanting eyes which are only attractive in the mystical and romantic Orient of novels, many Japanese American girls undergo eye operations to create a double fold of the eyelids or use scotch tape to make their eyes appear rounder and fuller.

The concern with eye-shape goes further than being just a female worry. One friend told me that she once went out on a date with a young man who was in one of her classes at the University. As he picked her up and they went out, she noticed something was peculiar about him. Not being able to pinpoint what was wrong, she forgot about it until they returned to her home. As he was kissing her goodnight, she then noticed what had been unusual. He was wearing scotch tape on his eyelids!

It also remains a very real fact of life that many Japanese American females are overly conscious about their bust size. Buying special creams and exercise apparatus which promise quick results, the flat-chested Japanese American female is often hung-up over the fact that she is not the lady with the big *chi-chis*. Despite the special bras with the scientifically designed contours which promise the wearer more attractive breasts, many females remain what some of their boyfriends would call "seriously deprived."

So besides having the normal preoccupations with pimples, dandruff and unwanted fat, some Japanese Americans in Hawaii feel a special need to alter certain aspects of their physical appearance. But overall, the Japanese American is not immersed in an environment where the ideals of beauty are racially unattainable. Indeed, what is locally considered beautiful to a large degree reflects many of the features of the Oriental. The long, straight black hair, the petite body, the flavor of Asian features in the face are all aspects of beauty with which the Japanese American can easily identify.

Therefore it is not uncommon that when you ask many locals, be they Asian, Polynesian or haole, who they feel are the most beautiful people in Hawaii they will respond "someone of mixed ancestry." That is, the Filipino-haole, the Japanese-Hawaiian or the Japanese-haole are the people who possess the best physical qualities of the different races. This response illustrates the intermingling of the most dramatic or attractive physical features of a people to produce a hybrid beauty unique to Hawaii.

What a Japanese American considers beautiful and what he looks for in terms of the physical appearance of a person is an ingredient of his self-identity. An understanding of sexual ideas, however, should also be concerned with the attitudes toward morality and the nature of sex within the ethnic group. It is the attitudes and morality toward sex which become guideposts by which an individual maintains and directs his life and by which he is judged.

To the outsider, Hawaii's people have frequently been imagined as natives in a sexual paradise. In the continual warmth of the Islands which know no winter or fall, among the many flora which provide tropical fruits in abundance, many people who have never been to Hawaii can still see in their minds the bronzed nude bodies of isle nymphs and the handsome natives frolicking freely in the surf or languishing under a palm tree, softly strumming their ukuleles. Morality, civilization and sexual frustration cannot exist, they reason, in a place so beautiful, so exotic.

Others see Hawaii in the image of a typical sailor haven. They expect to find in Honolulu prostitutes, pimps, sex shows and perversions which men seek after nine months at sea. And these people complain that if one visits Hotel Street, this image of a sailor's seaport is all too well reinforced.

But unfortunately, Island living isn't always such a sexual heaven or flesh-pot for its people. Although the ideal Polynesian-Oriental-haole beauties can be found in newspaper ads, romping on postcards and flashing across floorshows, the Islands are comprised of many peoples who possess diverse attitudes and beliefs concerning what is proper and improper sexual activity. Each ethnic group, and each social class within an ethnic group, has a different attitude toward sex and love. While the so-called "Noble Savage" could have enjoyed sex openly and freely in ancient times, Hawaii's people can no longer be so bluntly generalized. Although streetwalkers, *mahus* and pornography are found on Hotel Street, they are hardly typical of other areas in Honolulu, such as Kaimuki or Makiki.

Consequently, in Hawaii today, one finds a series of attitudes which are projected upon a group by themselves and others. For example, Hawaiians are occasionally portrayed in the media and in the minds of some people as being extremely sexually promiscuous. The males hang out at Waikiki Beach and play the role of "beachboys," teaching surfing and the fine art of love to rich, middle-aged women touring the Islands. Other males who are called "Primo Warriors" are frequently pictured as rapists of haole girls; they find no satiation for their sexual appetites.

In the same vein, Hawaiian females have been portrayed as loose and sexually free. Out-of-wedlock births, frequent marriages and divorces and constant pregnancies are some of the negative attitudes which are projected on the Hawaiians by other peoples. The question which must be asked, though, is how well do we understand the cultural factors which become grossly distorted by such stereotypes? What is the actual Hawaiian notion towards sex? In addition, it must be recognized that many Hawaiian families in no way can be identified with these negative perceptions.

By the same token, the notion that Filipino men are all "horny" must also be questioned. To what degree has the imbalance of male-female ratio in the Filipino community contributed to creating this local stereotype? And obviously, there are many Filipinos who are perfectly normal husbands without any of the wild-eyed, sex-starved desires which their stereotype would imply.

Again, when a local girl says she dates only haole men because they are good conversationalists and are suave, we must question the applicability of such an attitude. There are those haoles who are rough and rowdy without much surface *savoir-faire*. There are others who are completely involved in a middle-class life who initially would appear to have little of the romantic lover in them.

In short, the sexual beliefs held by ethnic groups about themselves and other groups in Hawaii cannot be applied indiscriminately, nor can they be applied without an understanding of the community factors involved. So when one talks about sexual attitudes of the Japanese American, one must avoid making blanket generalizations. The Japanese American, for example, is often pictured by himself and others as being a sexually boring middle-class dud. In the demanding life of middle-class living, with emphasis on studying or working hard, keeping the nose to the grindstone and "keeping out of debt," there is little time or opportunity for an exciting or varied sex life. Morals and values ranging from the newspaper pulp of Ann Landers or Abigail Van Buren to the deep beliefs and highly respected attitudes of religion are the cornerstone of their upbringing and world view.

For many Japanese Americans, the image of middle-class style of living, including the sexual attitude which characterizes that style, has become a fundamental way of life. If indeed the Japanese Americans are "out-whiting the white" in their pursuit of middle-class security, the same is true for the clean sexual image they project. Children are made to feel obligated to achieve in the classroom, not in bed. Girls are taught the necessary acts to become a good housewife, not a thrilling lover. Restrictions on the use of the family car, dating practices, curfew hours and other techniques of family control conform ideally with the virtues of the church, temple, Ms. Landers or Ms. Van Buren.

The result of the perpetuation of the middle-class modes of living casts a stereotype for the Japanese American which reflects neither an attitude of being "horny" and sexually promiscuous nor of being virile and debonaire. On a normal day at McKinley High School, observe the vast majority of Japanese American girls and boys who attend classes. Neatly dressed and scrubbed, hair clean and combed, they demonstrate the wholesome quality of good, normal youths. It is no wonder, then, that the Japanese American female is a "virgin" in the framework of the attitude of the middle class. Petite and demure, she is the epitome of the girl next door, the Pollyanna who naively knows nothing or ever hears anything about the world of sex and love. She is graceful, dainty, sweet, a lotus blossom, a lover of flower arrangements, tea ceremonies and babysitting.

And the Japanese American males also are sexually immature and therefore considered "nice." They have little if any experience with women nor do they have a sexy quality about them. They are more involved with studying, raising guppies in aquariums or playing basketball with friends than scoring with girls. They are the everlover of hobbies, cars and plate lunches.

Captured within this mystique of sexual inadequacy and inexperience, Japanese Americans supposedly become frustrated with their middle-class orientation towards love and sex. They see around them people and other ethnic groups which haven't the moral restrictions or sexual confusions which they perceive for themselves. "Why," they frustratedly ask their partners, "are you so much like me?"

So incomprehensible is the image of a Japanese American being sexually unrestricted that when good, middle-class children are exposed in perverse activities the entire community, Japanese and non-Japanese members alike, is shocked. One incident which typifies the strength of this Japanese American image of strict sexual middle-classness occurred on the Big Island in the late 1950s. About six Japanese American youths who represented "normal" Japanese boys and one Portuguese boy, gang-raped a Japanese American girl. The crime shook the Japanese American community of the Big Island both because of the shame involved and because of the actions of their children. Were they really interested in sex that badly? The rest of the community was amazed that the same ethnic group which produced excellent students and athletes could also produce rapists; that sort of crime could be expected only from other ethnic groups. "No doubt," many must have thought at the time, "the Pordagee put them all up to it."

The stereotype of the Japanese American couple being dull and inexperienced in the ways of love is also not always the case. This is especially true when one realizes that perhaps a Western criteria of love and sex is used when one analyzes the Japanese American. While on the surface a predominant attitude of sexual impotency emerges, perhaps within the Japanese American family different types of values are stressed, different behaviors rewarded, so that love and sex are cherished in a manner incomprehensible to others.

A striking example of love in the Japanese American

community which goes far beyond the stereotypic confines of middle class dullness is contained in a story related by Tsuneichi Yamamoto entitled "A Marriage in Heaven" which is repeated below:

> In Japan a double love suicide is called "consummation of a love in heaven." This point of view is incomprehensible to Westerners.
>
> They ask, "Why don't they get married if they are in love?"
>
> However, social customs and tradition oftentimes did not allow youngsters in love to get married. And those who dared to defy customs and/or parental opinion were looked upon as outcasts by others. Thus there were occasions when the only way left for couples in love was "to get married in heaven." And human nature being as it is, on the other hand, lauded the courage and determination of such couples who defied social restrictions and chose death as a means to attain their objective. This feeling has been reflected in the ever popular kabuki plays such as "Osome-Hisamatsu," "Umegawa-Chubei" and "The Love Suicides of Toribe Yama."
>
> The Waianae incident occurred during the early morning hours on May 23, 1919. The parties to the tragedy were Kaoru Uyeda (18) and Kenichi Okamoto (19). Both their fathers were fishermen. They lived in a fishing village on the shores of Waianae and were practically neighbors with only one house between their homes. They had known each other for the last three years and had been in love for the past one-and-a-half years.
>
> Kaoru was a beautiful, gentle girl who worked in the plantation fields every day and took care of the housework in place of her mother who was an invalid due to a serious eye ailment. She was a dutiful daughter and was well thought of by all the villagers.
>
> She was, however, born under a "very unfortunate

star.'' Her real father had left for the U.S. mainland when she was two years old and nothing had been heard from him since. Her mother and she had been left in the care of a friend, but her mother had died under tragic circumstances involving another man when Kaoru was only six years old.

Kaoru had then been adopted by the Uyeda couple who had no children of their own. Her foster mother took her to Japan the next year where she went to school for the next four years. She returned to Hawaii in 1912 when she was 11 years old. She was a so-called Hawaii-born "kibei.''

On the other hand, Kenichi was born in Japan and had arrived in Hawaii three years previously in 1916 at the age of 16. He worked at Waianae mill and was known as a very dutiful son who never spoke back to his father.

It was only natural that Kenichi and Kaoru, with their similar backgrounds, become friends and then lovers. But in the meantime, Kenichi's father had made plans for his only son's future. He had already chosen a wife for his son—a girl named Misuyo, from his home village in Japan. Kenichi was told about this after all arrangements had been completed. To Kenichi, it seemed as if his whole world was shattered! He couldn't think of marrying anyone except Kaoru.

Kenichi and Kaoru were placed in a difficult position. They did not know what to do. On the one hand they were bound by duty and obligations to their parents, while on the other, they could not think of a life without each other. Their only recourse was fulfillment of their love in the next world. After talking all night at the beach, they returned to Kaoru's home, their decision made. Both their fathers were out fishing that night.

It was 2:30 A.M. May 23, 1919. Kaoru made herself beautiful for her last journey. She wore her favorite kimono and brought a cup from the kitchen and placed it between them. They had nothing more to say to each other. In silence, they both wrote a short farewell note to their parents. Kenichi next emptied the acid he had brought into the cup. Kaoru drank the first half followed by Kenichi who drank the remaining portion.

A girl, 13 years old, who had been taking care of Kaoru's sick mother was sleeping in the next room. She awoke when she heard Kaoru and Kenichi moaning in agony. She yelled for help, but when the neighbors arrived the two were already unconscious. Kaoru died on her way to the Waipahu Hospital, followed by Kenichi who feebly said, "I am sorry," and breathed his last.

Their pathetic farewell note begged forgiveness of their parents. It also stated that they would be married in the next world and requested that they be buried in the same grave.

There were no radios those days, but the incident as reported in the papers created a sensation—especially in the Japanese community. A group of local actors, "Taisho Ichiza," immediately incorporated the event into a play and made the rounds of the islands. The play was a smash hit, inasmuch as it depicted an incident still fresh in the peoples' minds.

Subsequently a headstone engraved "We Shall be United Again," was erected by the Waianae Buddhist Youths' and Women's Associations with funds donated by the "Taisho Ichiza." It still stands there today in the Waianae Japanese cemetery and is remembered by old-timers who burn incense sticks before the headstone when the anniversary date of the suicide comes around.

Although a memory from the past, Kenichi and Kaoru still defy the stereotype of the Japanese American couple who are quiet, dull and unromantic. Their story reveals a different attitude toward sex and love with many cultural variants which is molded in the Japanese American community of Hawaii.

"We Shall be United Again." *Photo courtesy of Jerry Y. Fuji-oka, Light Inc.*

To take the stereotype of the Japanese American at face value, then, and conclude that one prevailing attitude succinctly explains the community notions toward sex and love is not accurate. A number of Japanese Americans, for example, view themselves and are viewed by others as being very sexually liberated. They don't appear to have any overly moralistic restrictions to sexual behavior. The men have homes in high-rise condominiums with a beautiful view and a bevy of girls; they drive expensive cars, subscribe to *Playboy* or *Penthouse* magazines, dress like a T.V. commercial and have a special knack for attracting stunning women. Also, there are females who see themselves as vivacious lovers; they feel no need to have just one boyfriend nor do they feel a compulsion to marry.

And then there are the great majority of middle-class, morally based Japanese Americans who view sex as restricted to marriage and only one, small aspect of their lives which should be kept private. Just like so many of their counterparts in the haole, Hawaiian, Chinese or Filipino communities, they are not particularly the most sexually exciting people in the world.

But it would be unrealistic to conclude that all middle-class Japanese American males and females are dissatisfied with each other sexually. In their own way, they are relatively stable and happy. If you go to the beach on any sunny day, you'll see masses of Japanese Americans enjoying each other's company regardless of sexual differences. They don't seem particularly worried over the morality or circumstances of their lives. Should we suppose that underneath the laughing veneer of joy, they are all miserably frustrated, just waiting to jump into bed with a sexy haole, Hawaiian or Filipino? Perhaps for some, this is true. But after thoughtful consideration and with an understanding of the Japanese American of Hawaii, such would not appear to be always the case. The Japanese American is not unlike other human beings who have learned to understand and place in perspective their frustrations, anxieties and disappointments, even when they are of a sexual nature.

Although sexual attitudes and the ideal of beauty are an important dimension of self-identity, it is not the only consideration which affects how Japanese Americans conduct their lives. Other factors come into play.

4
It's Just a Way of Life

To the individualistic, to the carefree, nothing could be more abhorrent than obligations. Being obliged to your parents, your friends, your wife or your children, is oftentimes like having a love affair. In the back of your mind is that haunting thought, hounding your waking hours, that what you are enjoying today, you'll have to pay for tomorrow, or the next day, or the next.

But there are many cultures of people, removed from the super-individualism of Western urban living, who actually embrace obligations as a fundamental aspect of life. They accept their obligations not grudgingly or reluctantly, but freely. For obligation to them is an important mechanism of human relations and a predictable basis of future security—whatever you give, will eventually be returned.

While many ethnic groups in Hawaii have an informal or non-contractual system of reciprocal obligation, the Japanese American has developed an obligatory relationship with intimate friends and relatives which is noted for both its frequency and formality.

When a Japanese American is given a gift you can rest assured that he will not feel comfortable until he has reciprocated in a like manner. I should stress that, rather than reciprocating in an informal or spontaneous gesture depending on mood, he gives his gifts, and receives them, according to an intricate pattern of established norms and procedures which have evolved from Japan.

From the Japanese cultural concept of *giri,* transmitted via the Issei to Hawaii, the Nisei, Sansei and Yonsei have learned the advantages and disadvantages of reciprocal gift-giving. *Giri* behavior is created out of a moral obligation to reciprocate what one person gives to another. It requires a high degree of formalization and explicitness between the parties of a transaction. R. P. Dore, a scholar of Japanese culture, provides in his book *City Life in Japan* the following example which illustrates this point:

> Mr. A called at the B's household for a friendly chat and brought a gift of a very special sort of watermelon. He said that he just happened to be passing the fruiterers and thought they would like it. The next day Mrs. B went to the fruiterers to enquire how much such a melon would cost. She was told between 300 and 350 yen. She thereupon took to the A's a return gift of two bottles of beer, costing aproximately 250 yen. She explained that as A had brought the gift of his own accord the return gift should be of slightly less value than the original gift, but if she had asked A to get the melon for her it would have had to be considerably more expensive.

The earliest expressions of *giri* found among the Issei in Hawaii were on the plantation. Feeling a loyalty to their superiors and a responsibility to give gifts in return

Reciprocal giving of time and energy to help one's friends and neighbors is a way of life in Hawaii. *Photo courtesy of the Hawaii State Archives.*

for special favors, many times·the Issei used their money to pay for elaborate presents given the *luna* or plantation owner. It is recorded that one plantation manager was reluctant to send Christmas cards to his Japanese laborers because they would send him foods, boxes of cigars or other expensive items in return. With the wages of a plantation laborer in those early years, such reciprocity was at the expense of one's own welfare.

But it must be remembered that what was critical to the Issei's concept of *giri* was not the immediate rewards of a big bank account or an abundant dinner table, but fulfilling a *moral* obligation to repay kindness with kindness. And it cannot be taken that these actions were foolishly self-depreciatory or naively stupid. For what a person was to give away today, he could expect to be returned to him later. If you gave a family food or shelter so that they wouldn't starve or catch pneumonia from the dampness, then you could rightfully expect the same treatment when you were in the same dire circumstances. In a community where obligation and reciprocity are recognized as normal everyday patterns, a balanced human eco-system of cooperative effort and mutual assistance is established.

What the Issei transported to Hawaii and practiced on the plantation has remained in one form or another until today. You can find in the Japanese American community of Hawaii some very strong cultural practices of reciprocal obligation in a manner well-befitting *giri*. Tempered by an American outlook of "look out for number one," many times shunned as a silly custom, *giri* has survived and is still expressed in many aspects of the Japanese American lifestyle.

For example, on any weekend around the family

home in Kaimuki or Aiea, you can notice a group of men painting a house, building a stone wall or planting a lawn. Or you might see a group of women cooking a huge meal for a family gathering, preparing the lanai with decorations for a child's birthday party or helping to make a thousand paper cranes for a wedding. If you inquire, you'll find that these men and women are not of the same household, but are close friends and relatives who have offered to give their help for a special event or chore. Though their own house might need to be painted or their yard need to be cleaned that weekend, they are at their friend's home giving time and energy.

And if you look a couple of weeks later, perhaps you'll see the owner of the house which was painted under the hood of his friend's car adjusting the timing. Or you'll see the mother of the birthday girl at her friend's home helping to make *sushi*. In both cases, you have witnessed a form of reciprocal assistance which is commonly taken for granted in the Japanese American community. You have witnessed vestiges of the *giri* system of Japan operative in Hawaii.

But an example which really exemplifies the reciprocal system of obligation is found in the local bars and drinking establishments frequented by Japanese Americans. Imagine a group of four Nisei friends sitting at a table in a Kapahulu bar drinking Olympia or Primo beer. When they sit down, each takes ten dollars out of his pocket and places it on the table. Each of them realizes that it is his obligation to pay for the rounds of drinks until they have no money left or until they must stagger to their cars. No one at the table counts the number of drinks, tallies the bill or quibbles about spending too much money. This just isn't the "local" thing to do and you would be considered a *manjū* (a not so polite word equivalent to "tightwad") if you failed to put out.

By exposing the money on the table the hostess, whom you would most likely already know, would be given the necessary cue that you intended to do some pretty heavy drinking. Consequently she would bring to your table along with the drinks, a wide range of *pupus* or plates of food, depending on how well she knew you and how much money you put down. In its truest form, *giri* is found in this activity. The hostess has to pay for the food she brings you and she does not ask for any money to cover the cost of *sashimi,* steak, fried chicken, *ogo,* crab and egg omelet.

But the hostess is anticipating two things. First, because of her gift of *pupus,* you will leave her a tip which covers her expenditures. Secondly, and more importantly, that because of her gestures you will return and become a steady customer. This is not only beneficial to you, as you will be receiving good service and plenty of good *pupus,* but will be beneficial to the hostess who will build a steady business.

In addition, it will be beneficial because not only is an obligation formed, but it is an obligation which enriches the human relationship. You are not just a customer *vis-à-vis* a waitress, but you are both personal friends. The reward lies not only in the money and food but in the creation of intimate interpersonal relations.

Once you understand and appreciate this system, then the Japanese American psyche becomes immensely more comprehensible. For instance, I have a haole friend who cannot for the life of him break away from the value he places on saving his money. Blaming a mixture of Scottish and Jewish bloods, he is the first to recognize that he is a "penny pincher." Now when he goes drinking, he doesn't put any money on the table for fear of sticky fingers or unnatural gusts of wind. He tips a straight 10 percent. Yet he is still puzzled why all his Japanese friends receive good *pupus,* while he keeps getting peanuts in the shell.

So within the community, the Japanese American learns the subtle forms of obligation which not only facilitate his bar life but which enhance his relationships with others. The most important and primary form of *giri* which must be learned, however, is the practice of gift-giving among Japanese Americans. Gifts, usually in the form of money, are given for births, birthdays, confirmations, weddings, graduations from high school and college, sicknesses, trips, anniversaries, retirements and the last gift of them all, funerals. Within a Japanese American family, from grandparents, parents, children, aunties and uncles, to cousins, nephews, nieces and in-laws, from intimate friends and their children to associates and acquaintances, an enormous amount of gifts is being exchanged every month.

And in addition, what has been received must be remembered; a gift of equal value must be returned at some later birth, birthday, confirmation, graduation, wedding and *ad infinitum.*

Let us take a closer look at the way *giri* affects the lifestyle of the Japanese American, and consequently his identity, by looking at the custom of marriage. Marriage is signified in Hawaii as in most Judeo-Christian-Buddhist social environments by a wedding ceremony. And as is common for most weddings, a reception is held whereby guests are invited and nine course Chinese dinners are served.

The first chore of obligation for the potential bride

and groom is to determine who in the past had invited them to their weddings. Not only must the customary guests be invited, family and close friends, but those who had once invited either the bride or groom to a wedding. To neglect these former gestures of friendship would be an immediate violation of the code of obligation.

As guests bring gifts of money, toasters or rice-cookers to the reception, each present is duly recorded. At this point begin the procedures which I must sincerely say appear to be very important for Japanese Americans. After the money is counted, each gift is appraised as to its monetary worth. Then the mother and father of both the bride and groom judiciously go over the list of gifts and determine whether the guests have kept up their obligations. For example, "Did the Ogawas give a gift to our daughter which was equivalent to the gift we gave their son on his wedding?"

Now this listing of gifts and givers is kept as a handy reference for future use. When the bride and groom are invited to a wedding of someone on the list, they will know exactly the cost of their obligation. They must fulfill this obligation if they are to "save face" in the classic Japanese tradition.

In terms of the obligations which must be fulfilled and the obligations in the future which must be met, a Japanese American wedding can be a very trying affair. Picture, if you will, the honeymoon night, as the couple mulls over the list of guests and gifts which has just doubled the extent of their obligations for the many years to come. You can imagine why it is said that if a couple can survive the wedding, they have a good chance of surviving any marital problem.

The practice of reciprocal gift-giving is also evident in

other ways. A Japanese American decides to take a trip to Japan for instance. As he waits to board the airplane, bedecked with *leis* and saying good-bye to close relatives and friends, he is given what in Japanese is called *senbetsu*. *Senbetsu* is the practice of placing money in an envelope and giving it to a traveler just before departure.

At the time of the giving of *senbetsu* a little ritual is performed. The giver puts the envelope in the traveler's hands and urges, "Take it; only little bit." The traveler responds, "Oh, you shouldn't have done it," knowing full well he should have. The giver modestly smiles and shrugs, "Oh don't be silly."

After this courtesy is completed, the *senbetsu* is graciously accepted. But the obligation is not fulfilled until the traveler does one of two things. Either he can buy the giver a souvenir in the land to which he travels or he can remember the amount of the *senbetsu* and reciprocate when the giver himself takes a trip.

While giving the *senbetsu* is a very loving gesture and should be so interpreted, it can also be quite burdensome. That is, a person with many friends can find that he has purchased more souvenirs than can be allowed through U.S. Customs. Or he will realize that too much of his trip was spent shopping for gifts and carrying the merchandise everywhere he went. Even a short weekend trip from Oahu to an outer island such as Maui could result in boxes of *mochi,* Lahaina *nasubi* (if you can get it) and Maui onions having to be carried home to friends and relatives to whom one is obligated.

Another form of obligation, traceable to *giri,* is the phenomenon which I would call the "Plasticware Party"* syndrome. Not confined to only Japanese Ameri-

*A pseudonym for a popular kitchenware.

cans, the symptoms of this condition are appearing in greater frequency throughout the Islands among housewives. The syndrome begins when a housewife decides to hold a "Plasticware Party." During this party, consisting of about ten to twenty women, it is expected that each guest will buy some kind of household goods made of a synthetic durable plastic. The women eat potato chips and dip, "talk story" and order what they need in the line of cups, bowls, juice containers and salad molds. If a certain amount of goods is sold, then the hostess of the party will receive a special gift.

Sounds simple, doesn't it? It's not. After the party, the intricate webs of obligation which could approach a level of utter insanity begin to be spun. Each of the guests will usually host her own "Plasticware Party," so naturally everyone is re-invited to another home. To attend the party becomes your obligation. At each party the guests must purchase an equivalent amount of goods to the amount which was purchased at their party. So if Mrs. Masuda had gone to Mrs. Nagano's party and spent $10, Mrs. Nagano would have to spend $10 at Mrs. Masuda's party. Now with ten people involved you can see the obligatory madness. One ends up buying goods which one doesn't need, use or in any way desire.

But it doesn't stop with the first party. Special and more expensive gifts are given with the more parties you host. So the level of insanity mounts as each participant re-invites the same people to buy what at times are useless goods, thus fulfilling the obligations of previous parties. What you must spend at each party, based on the amount which the hostess spent at your party, becomes an engrained accountbook in the minds of countless housewives.

And who suffers from this "Plasticware Party" syndrome? The husband. As one desperate husband lamented, "I am sick of this kind junk. Every cupboard I open, plasticware, plasticware, plasticware, dishes, cups, containers and more containers. I haven't eaten off a hard plate in months."

Indeed, it takes many months for a housewife to regain her senses and gracefully disinvolve herself from the network of "Plasticware Parties" in which she is trapped. Politely she must meet all of her obligations but at the same time not create any new ones.

While providing a source of humor and good-natured fun, the syndrome of the "Plasticware Party" is a distinctly Hawaiian event. Only in the cultural atmosphere of Hawaii where obligation is an integral part of the lifestyles of so many ethnic groups, can women become so intensely involved in such extended activities.

The final example which illustrates the forms of obligation found among Japanese Americans is the custom associated with funerals. At typical American funerals a mourner expresses his condolences through the offering of flowers. At the Japanese American funeral flowers are replaced by the giving of *kōden*. Crisp, new bills placed in a clean white envelope, the *kōden* is given to the deceased's family as a way to defray the expenses of the funeral. The amount of money depends on the closeness of the families or the size of the *kōden* which the mourner might have received previously from the deceased's family. If reciprocating a previous *kōden,* it is in bad taste to give more or less than what was originally given.

All the money received is carefully recorded in terms of obligations which have been fulfilled or new ones created. At times the deceased's family gives to mourners small gifts such as a book of stamps or tea. For people close to the family a dinner or lunch is arranged after the funeral.

The sociological importance of the Japanese American funeral as an occasion for reaffirming obligatory relationships and engaging in common bereavement is indicated by the Japanese newspapers and radio. The Japanese obituaries in the newspapers and those regularly announced over radio serve as an information service to Japanese Americans who want to be kept informed of recent deaths and scheduled services. Since it is shame for a Japanese American not to attend a friend's or relative's funeral, it is essential that he check newspapers and radios so that none are overlooked. For the Issei especially, as friends and family die, the funeral is a symbolic gesture which cannot be forgotten.

So while *giri* can be a source of involved entanglements almost humorously self-defeating, it can also be an ethnic bond of mutual identity among Japanese Americans. The involvement you feel with your community of friends and relatives is based not on your whims of civic-mindedness or innate goodwill but is an emanation of the moral obligation you have toward other human beings.

In the rural communities of Japan in the nineteenth century *giri* served as a vital mechanism which brought people together in a secure, self-perpetuating common spirit. *Giri* provided for a basis of mutually predictive behavior so that cooperation and assistance could protect the members of a village community. During times of crisis, illness, starvation or incapacity, one could rely on the aid of one's neighbors because it was their moral obligation to provide help.

In Hawaii during the early plantation experience when the Issei sought to develop their own rural community away from Japan, *giri* again played an essential role in the organization and patterning of interpersonal relations. The individual Issei, alone, would not have been able to survive on the plantation without the cooperation and obligation of his friends and relatives.

And even in the more modern and urban settings of Hawaii, removed from the plantation and the Meiji Era of land peasantry, the Japanese American has retained in his own way the practice of obligation. This retention is notable considering that within the Westernized social system of Hawaii an individual does not have to rely on the obligations of his friends and relatives for needed social services. Welfare, old age pensions, unemployment insurance, health and life insurance are institutions established to protect the individual from the uncertainties of the future and make notions of obligation less important.

Yet despite this fact of American urbanization, obligation is still an integral part of the life and identity of Japanese Americans in Hawaii. It is not the final wispy utterances of a dying custom but an unconscious value of daily life. Indeed, if one were to ask a Japanese American why they bother to maintain these small traditions they might respond simply that it's just a way of life.

And this way of life performs some very real functions in the community. *Giri* still retains in the Hawaii of today its fundamental human purposes. Through the acts of obligation, in gift-giving and offering freely one's time and talents to friends and relatives, the Japanese American is daily reaffirming the intimate human relationships in which he is involved. The reason why *giri* still thrives in the community is because it goes beyond the money or presents to what in Japanese is called *kimochi,* a feeling from the heart. In a world which the disenchanted say is becoming more impersonal and alienating, *giri* makes relationships between people more meaningful by preserving the intimacy and cohesiveness of human groups.

To conclude, I cannot deny that there are those Sansei who express their consternation and disappointment with the obligation of their parents. I can recall one student, for example, who complained to me, "My mom made me save all my graduation money so I could give it away to all my relatives who are graduating." I cannot also deny that there are those Sansei who see gift-giving as a chance to reap a fortune. Not comprehending the reciprocity involved, the lavishness of their relatives on graduation, before trips or on birthdays is seen as a means of saving up for a surfboard or putting a down payment on a new Volkswagen.

Yet even these Sansei, who look upon obligations as a nuisance or a way of making money, continue *giri* in their own way. Before going to a party, they stop at the market to buy dessert or some *pupus;* they never go empty-handed and expect the same from their friends. In the true tradition of the Islands, they still show obligation and mutual respect to others, which is their heritage of *giri.*

5
A Legacy of Everlasting Importance

Sundays at Kapiolani Park in 1919 were hardly the aristocratic and opulent events that they had been when Hawaii was still a monarchy and the park had been the royal playground. But ideally situated near Waikiki, under the gaze of Diamond Head Crater, Kapiolani was still the scene of polo games, horse races, and the gatherings of the very best *kamaaina* families of Honolulu.

On the Sunday of March 16, 1919, Kapiolani Park was transformed into the backdrop for a symbolic event in the history of Japanese-Hawaiian relations. Five years earlier Emperor Yoshihito, the one hundred twenty-third Emperor of the Empire of the Rising Sun, had been crowned in Tokyo. In commemoration of the Emperor's coronation, the Japanese of Hawaii on this Sunday were to present to the City and County of Honolulu a modified duplicate of a fountain in Hibiya Park, Tokyo.

Among the prominent guests who attended the unveiling of what was called "Phoenix Fountain" were Governor of the Territory of Hawaii C. J. McCarthy, Mayor of Honolulu J. J. Fern, president and speaker of the Territorial Legislature and thousands of Japanese. The official presentation of the "Phoenix Fountain" was conducted by Consul General Rokurō Moroi of Japan, who announced that the fountain was a "testimonial of friendship and equality of the Japanese residing in the Hawaiian Islands."

The fountain was draped in the national colors of *Dai Nippon*. Following a prayer by a Shinto priest, the drapery was drawn aside and the fountain, reflecting the intense glare of the morning heat, flashed out like the rays of the sun causing spectators to shield their eyes. Then, with great enthusiasm, the traditional *banzais* were shouted as the peoples of Hawaii and Japan proclaimed mutual friendship and trust. For as one Japanese speaker noted, "We are assembled here to mark a spot of everlasting importance in the annals of the history of the Japanese people of Hawaii."

Today, if you go to Kapiolani Park to see the "spot of everlasting importance," the "testimonial of friendship and equality," you will be sadly disappointed. A victim of the emotional turmoil and racial animosity generated by World War II, "Phoenix Fountain" was destroyed in 1943, its metal casting turned into scrap. Jubilantly the *Honolulu Advertiser* reported, on the first anniversary of the attack upon Pearl Harbor, that the "fountain which stood in Kapiolani Park for 25 years as a public symbol of Japanese imperialism may at last be removed."

As a fitting tribute the scrap metal of the fountain was to be returned to Japan. "The suitability of the metal for scrap," the *Advertiser* wrote, "which might be sent back to Japan in a form similar to the tokens of esteem which fell on Pearl Harbor Dec. 7, 1941, will be decided after it is dismantled."

"Phoenix Fountain," a spot of everlasting importance in the history of the Japanese people of Hawaii. *Photo courtesy of the Wakukawa Collection.*

A group of individuals sharing a common culture or heritage also inherit a common history, a history often replete with bitter irony. As that history evolves through the generations and is tempered by various social, economic and political factors, a group attitude or self-identity emerges. Reflecting hostility, love, superiority or inferiority towards others, the identity which the past thrusts upon the present is an important determinant of the role which a group will play in society and how it will view itself and others.

For the Japanese Americans of Hawaii, the past has usually been interpreted as being one of conflict, hatred and struggle. It was a negative experience of plantation slavery, social ostracism, outright condemnation and paranoid fear. Consequently, according to this viewpoint, the Japanese American has developed an identity based on a nightmare past which makes him fearful of other races in the community, too willing to show deference to authority and complacent in what some have called their American brainwashing.

But as in any human experience, there is another side, another legacy of the past besides that of oppression. Concurrent with the negative aspects of the Japanese American past and in part helping to explain the position which this ethnic group has attained in Hawaii's community, has been the influence of mutual respect and equality between ethnic groups. Although symbolically destroyed in 1943, the friendship and equality between Japan and Hawaii typified in the "Phoenix Fountain" preceded the unreasonable hatred and racial inequality which was encountered by the Japanese immigrant. And in many ways, the natural affinity between Japan and Hawaii has been more prevalent in shaping the attitudes which Japanese Americans have toward themselves and others in Hawaii.

Much has been written about the *aloha* spirit which has characterized race relations in Hawaii, and many have exposed such a spirit as a false front for more insidious racial and cultural discrimination. While one cannot escape the racially-based treatment given plantation laborers, the suspicions and paranoias, one also cannot escape the unalterable conclusion that the

Japanese in Hawaii view their past as a beneficial experience; they feel that they have enjoyed a friendly and inviting atmosphere marked with a movement towards equality.

Indeed, if you are to understand the meaning of the word "local," which is usually used as a common means of identification among long-term residents of mostly non-haole racial ancestry, then you must understand that the history of the Japanese American hasn't been one of only hardship and racial distrust. Certain levels of respect and trust had developed between the people of Japan and Hawaii from the earliest time so that Japanese and their children could openly, and at times lovingly, identify with being a part of the Hawaiian society. Such respect and friendliness to some measure forestalled the emotional outbursts that marred California in World War II and paved the way for the participation of Japanese in the Hawaiian economy and government in the post war years. To understand the legacy of friendship which has bound the Japanese and the people of Hawaii, to discover the roots of amiability, we must return to a nostalgic era of Hawaii and Japan, when Emperors and Kings still held sway over the affairs of state and royalty still stirred the hearts of men.

The dock was still damp from the rain the night before and the rising sun did little to warm the chilly morning of January 20, 1881. The early risers who had come to watch the Hawaiian King leave on his trip around the world crowded near the "City of Sydney," straining to see the royal entourage and to bid a personal farewell to their "Merry Monarch."

It was six o'clock in the morning when the gangplank

was finally pulled back, the hawsers cut loose, and the great steamer moved out to sea. As the Royal Band played "Home Sweet Home" a multitude of handkerchiefs on ship and shore waved their final *alohas*. Those on the wharf near the aft of the ship where the King stood, said that tears rolled down his cheeks and so they began to weep also. On the ship's main the Royal Standard flew and the still Honolulu morning was filled with the roar of the Punchbowl Guns saluting the King's departure.

King David Kalakaua, the beloved Monarch of the Hawaiian Kingdom, was in his seventh year of reign in 1881. Succeeding King Lunalilo, who had left no heir apparent to the throne, Kalakaua was the second Hawaiian King who had to be elected from among the various chiefs, or *aliis*. His election victory in 1874, defeating Queen Emma, goddaughter of Queen Victoria and the leading churchwoman of the Anglican church, was not received wholeheartedly by the entire populace. The contest and campaign propaganda had been bitter and fierce, and rioting broke out in the streets of Honolulu when supporters of Queen Emma received the news of Kalakaua's victory.

Equally discomfited were many American haoles residing in Hawaii. Kalakaua was an able politician who could skillfully judge situations. As leader of the "Young Hawaiians," a militant political party, he could be a promoter of the notion of "Hawaii for the Hawaiians." And yet in other circumstances, he could cooperate with Americans. For example, in the year of his election he journeyed to Washington to negotiate the Reciprocity Treaty which was the foundation of the successful sugar industry in Hawaii and brought prosperity throughout his reign. Deeply loyal and committed to his people, Kalakaua's primary interest was the independence and autonomy of the Hawaiian monarchy from foreign powers which made him unpredictable. "My earnest desire," he announced at the time of his candidacy for the kingship, "is for the perpetuity of the crown and the permanent independence of the government and people of Hawaii."

Fearful of Kalakaua's dubious political ambitions and alleged dislike for Americans, the contempt and distrust of prominent haole leaders were aroused. Attorney General Albert F. Judd was alleged to have said that he "would almost prefer the chances of a revolution, to the nomination of Colonel Kalakaua." Theo Davies, British acting commissioner, said of Kalakaua that "he is a man of fair education, little intelligence, and I fear no principle. He is supremely Hawaiian in his sympathies, bitterly opposed to American missionaries and people, and shows a great friendship and regard for Great Britain." "The natives will elect Kalakaua," wrote Davies on another occasion, "but the Americans will do *anything* to prevent his election."

The "City of Sydney" took King Kalakaua to San Francisco, accompanied by Chamberlain Charles H. Judd and Attorney General William N. Armstrong. Ten days later he boarded the "Oceanic" for the Pacific voyage to Japan. The motives behind the King's global voyage were both for official and personal reasons. There were indications that the King was seeking confirmation of the immigration of foreign laborers for the sugar plantations, strongly supported by the fact that Armstrong was also travelling as Commissioner of Immigration. Some felt that the King simply was curious to see the different cultures and peoples of the world. He had announced before a congregation of his native subjects at Kawaiahao Church that the object of his trip was first to recuperate his health and second, to find a means to recuperate his people through the introduction of a healthy population of foreign immigrants.

There is no record of what King Kalakaua had expected to accomplish in Japan. It is known that he was travelling incognito as "Alii Kalakaua" and had intended to secure lodging in a Yokohama hotel. Without intending to be recognized as the King of Hawaii, he must have had little ambition of doing serious diplomatic negotiations in Japan. However, if Kalakaua was truly seeking a source of immigrant labor to the Hawaiian Islands, then he and his American advisers must have been very anxious about the possibility of establishing a mutually profitable rapport with the Imperial Government of Japan.

As the sun hovered over the Bay of Yedo and a glimmer of snow-clad "Mt. Fusyama" could be seen to the west, the "Oceanic" arrived at Yokohama, Japan, on March 4. Unbeknownst to the King and his suite, officials in San Francisco had wired ahead to Tokyo to announce that the Monarch of the Hawaiian Islands was to visit Japan. Prepared then for the King's arrival, 42 men-of-war and large steamers anchored in the bay, representing ships from Russia, Britain, France and Japan, raised their bunting flags, and every one flew from their main truck the Hawaiian flag. As the "Oceanic" passed each ship a small ritual was repeated. A 21 gun royal salute would ring out from the bow of each foreign ship and the Royal Standard on the mainmast of the "Oceanic" would dip in response while King Kalakaua, standing dignified, would lift his hat to each ship he passed.

When the "Oceanic" anchored, hundreds of sampans and small crafts of all kinds swarmed about the steamer. The people on board the boats were making a great din by shouting so that even the "Oceanic's" steam whistle could not be heard above all the noise. Finally a distant battery blast and a puff of smoke signalled the approach of the steam launch "Mikado" carrying a forked white flag with a red ball in the center, over which was a royal crown. At the nearing of the "Mikado" which carried Admiral Nakamura of the Royal Japanese Navy, the swarming sampans began to paddle out of sight.

Admiral Nakamura boarded the "Oceanic," approached Kalakaua's suite and conveyed His Imperial Majesty's wish that his Royal brother of Hawaii be the guest of the Emperor of Japan during the King's stay on Japanese soil. Expecting to travel incognito, Kalakaua and his companions were hardly dressed in the manner befitting royalty. Negligently clothed, needing a bath, the Hawaiian King remained impassive as he entered the Japanese war boat which took him and his suite to the Emperor's summer palace at Yokohama, the Noge-yama.

The reception accorded Kalakaua in the streets of Yokohama was no less enthusiastic than that which he had been given in the Bay of Yedo. The streets they travelled were draped on either side with Japanese and Hawaiian flags, suspended from lofty poles. The entourage rode in an imperial carriage sent from Tokyo to serve the King of Hawaii, the first King of Christendom to step on Japanese soil. Troops and citizens lined the streets, unexpectedly silent and stolid, curiously watching the uncommon spectacle while the bands played the Japanese national anthem and *Hawaii Ponoi*.

Arriving at the summer palace, the King and his suite

were accommodated in magnificent chambers decorated with Japanese art, but supplied with European furniture and bedding. The chairs and drawers were ebony and gold; palatial chandeliers hung from the ceilings and the surfaces of the tables and doors were burnished gold and glossy lacquered enamel. The King reportedly said of his Japanese reception and accommodations, "*Maikai no!*" (Very good).

The next morning at 11 o'clock, the Royal visitors dressed now in full regalia, left Yokohama by express train for Tokyo for an audience with the Emperor. Arriving after an 18-mile, one-hour ride, the Royal entourage was then escorted to the Imperial Palace, passing crowds of bowing, silent and inquisitive Japanese.

As the King and his suite neared Akasaka, the palace of the Emperor, a bugle announced their arrival. The Emperor Meiji of Japan, stood alone in a room adjacent to the entrance of the palace. He was dressed in European military uniform and the crest of his coat was decorated with orders. As Kalakaua left the carriage and entered the palace, he stepped up to the Emperor alone and extended his arm to shake hands. For the first time in Japanese history an Emperor exchanged handshakes with a foreign sovereign.

After greeting the Imperial Empress who was dressed in the traditional *kimono*, he conferred with the Emperor for 20 minutes with the aid of a translator. Then King Kalakaua, Chamberlain Judd and Attorney General Armstrong re-entered the Imperial carriage and returned to their residence, the palace of Enriokwan. As was the custom of monarchical etiquette, a royal visit was to be returned by the Emperor within an hour. Consequently, as Kalakaua began to settle into his chambers, a bugler announced that the Emperor was

For the first time in Japanese history, an emperor had ex-changed handshakes with a foreign sovereign. King Kalaka-ua, his advisers, and Japanese diplomats in Japan. *Photo courtesy of the Hawaii State Archives.*

approaching the palace. Again the King of Hawaii and the Emperor of Japan briefly conferred. After the Emperor left, a series of Imperial Princes, foreign ambassadors and the American ambassador in Japan paid their respects to the visiting King at lunches, teas and dinners which continued throughout the day and evening.

King Kalakaua had intended to spend three days in Japan, but by request of the Emperor who wished to entertain his guest with a royal banquet, a grand ball, a review of the Imperial troops and special theatrical exhibitions, his stay was extended to ten days. During that time, Kalakaua visited Buddhist temples, memorials, museums, the naval academy and factories. Later, Kalakaua even received a copy of the New Testament in the Japanese language from a group of Japanese Christians in Yokohama whose church had been partially built with aid from Hawaiian Christians.

In addition to playing the royal sightseer, the King during his ten days in Japan made three far sighted proposals which established between Hawaii and Japan a natural friendship and equality which were to be the basis for Japanese immigration to Hawaii and the attitude which Japanese were to have towards Hawaii and Hawaiians.

Since her exposure to the Western world, Japan had been subjected to humiliation and subjugation by European powers who had sought to develop this newly opened Asiatic market as a profitable source of goods and resources. As stipulated in Japan's treaties with foreign nations, countries having trade with Japan were granted extra-territorial rights. This degrading policy gave to foreign nations sovereignty over a number of Japan's own seaports, called "treaty ports," in violation of international law. These "treaty ports" would be administered by foreign consuls, often incompetent, who were the final authorities in all matters concerning Japanese. The treaties were written and agreed to at a time when Japan was a weak and ineffectual power, and the foreign powers refused to abrogate the treaties or the extra-territorial rights granted them despite the earnest request of the Imperial Government.

When Kalakaua visited Japan in 1881, he too represented a nation which had special privileges of extra-territoriality as established by a most-favored-nation clause in the treaty of 1871 between Japan and Hawaii. But Kalakaua was prepared to win the favor of the Japanese Government so as to induce Japanese immigration by doing what was necessary to establish cordial and profitable relations between the two Kingdoms of the Pacific.

Consequently, in formal meetings with the Imperial Government and with the agreement of Judd and Armstrong, Kalakaua offered to relinquish Hawaii's rights to extra-territoriality, an unprecedented gesture of friendship. When Count Inouye of the Imperial Court was informed of the King's appreciation for the reception given him and his intentions to respond by abrogating the harsh and unjust clause of the 1871 treaty, the Count joyfully responded that this would be a red-letter day in Japanese history.

Although Kalakaua's proposal was well-received by Japan, the abrogation of the extra-territorial rights was never executed. When the European nations learned of the Hawaiian King's ambitions in a Japan-Hawaii rapprochement, they strenuously objected. Such a recognition by Hawaii of Japan's right to sovereignty over her own ports would seriously dent the European treaty system with which Europeans controlled Japan. As Attorney General Armstrong was to remark, the Europeans must have exclaimed in private, "Oh, bother the little Hawaiian beggar for getting between our legs."

In spite of the fact that Kalakaua's first proposal was never actualized, its impact in cementing good relations between Japan and Hawaii was significant. But the two other proposals went even further.

During one of the many gala receptions entertaining the royal visitors, King Kalakaua excused himself and proceeded to pay a secret visit to the Emperor at his palace. It was the evening of March 10 when the

Emperor, thinking something was peculiar about such an unannounced Royal *tête-à-tête,* received the Hawaiian monarch.

The purpose of the King's secret meeting with the Emperor was to present his other two proposals, which he realized would create a bond between Japan and Hawaii but which his American advisers would vehemently oppose. First, Kalakaua expressed to the Emperor the problems Hawaii was having with foreign interference, problems not unlike those of Japan. The government was beset with problems involving the presence of foreign powers which threatened Hawaii's independence. To remedy the situation, and to enlist the help of Japan, Kalakaua reiterated his request that Japan allow extensive labor immigration to Hawaii. Then the King proposed a royal alliance between the Kingdoms of Hawaii and Japan. During his visit to the Naval Academy, Kalakaua had met a 15-year-old Japanese Prince, Yamashina Sadamaro, later known as Prince Komatsu, with whom he was duly impressed. He proposed that the prince and his niece, Princess Kaiulani, then five years old and supposedly Kalakaua's choice as his successor to the throne, be married.

Then to secure a counterbalance of power against the American encroachment in Hawaii, Kalakaua made an even more extraordinary suggestion. Recognizing the tenuous positions both Japan and Hawaii were in *vis-à-vis* Europe and America, Kalakaua proposed the formation of a "Union and Federation of Asiatic nations and sovereigns." The only evidence of Kalakaua's proposal is contained in a letter written from the Emperor to the King at a later date.

While Your Majesty was in my capital, you have in course of conversation alluded to a Union and Federa-

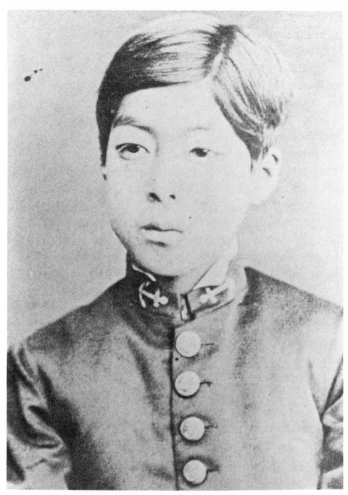

During his visit to the naval academy, King Kalakaua had met fifteen-year-old Prince Komatsu with whom he was duly impressed. *Photo from Ralph S. Kuykendall,* The Hawaiian Kingdom, *vol. 3 (Honolulu: University of Hawaii Press, 1967). Courtesy of The University Press of Hawaii.*

King Kalakaua proposed that Princess Kaiulani, five years old and Kalakaua's supposed choice as heir apparent, be married to Prince Komatsu. *Photo courtesy of the Hawaii State Archives.*

tion of the Asiatic nations and sovereigns. I highly agree with Your Majesty's profound and farseeing views. Your Majesty was also good enough to state that I might be the promoter and chief of this Federation. I cannot but be grateful for such expression of your love and confidence in me.

The Oriental nations including my country have long been in a state of decline and decay; and we cannot hope to be strong and powerful unless by gathering inches and treasuring foots gradually restore to us all attributes of a nation. To do this our Eastern Nations ought to fortify themselves within the walls of such Union and Federation, and by uniting their power to endeavor to maintain their footing against those powerful nations of Europe and America, and to establish their independence and integrity in future. To do this is a pressing necessity for Eastern Nations, and in so doing depend their lives.

The Emperor was struck by the importance of the proposals and their international impact. He promised to give them serious consideration. Following this evening of private negotiations, the King hid the nature of his secret visit with the Emperor from his advisers. But through Japanese sources, the suite learned of the King's midnight wandering and Armstrong wrote that "it made the suite more watchful against escapades of the Crowned Head it was steering around the world."

After a startling earthquake which the Japanese hosts accustomed to such tremors hardly acknowledged, a royal visit to the theater and a royal banquet interrupted by the news of the assassination of the Tsar of Russia, King Kalakaua left Yokohama on March 16. It had been an impressive and memorable visit to Japan for the Monarch of the Hawaiian Islands. As a final gesture of gratitude, the Emperor invested Kalakaua with the Grand Cross of the Order of the Rising Sun, and lesser grades on Armstrong and Judd. Kalakaua in return bestowed upon the Emperor the Grand Cross of the Order of Kamehameha I which had to be specially ordered from Paris where such royal medals were minted.

Of the Japanese visit and King Kalakaua, the Japanese press expressed mixed reactions. Some criticized the Imperial Government for wasting its time and money on such an insignificant King from such an insignificant Kingdom. Others blasted Kalakaua as simply a stooge of the United States, unworthy of extraordinary attention. Of his plans to seek Japanese immigration, the *Japanese Gazette* stated that "if King Kalakaua is on a visit to this country with the ostensible intention of inducing Japanese to desert the broad acres here . . . and go with him to a country of which they know nothing . . . His Majesty [should] see the fruitlessness and utter absurdity of asking the people to abandon the vast natural wealth undeveloped in Japan."

The press also reported Kalakaua in a favorable light. The *Japan Daily Mail* said of Kalakaua that "he is about the middle height, thickset, but of really handsome personal appearance. His complexion is not darker than that of an ordinary Japanese." To the criticism that Kalakaua did not deserve the attention he received, the *Daily Mail* replied that "if His Majesty were a cannibal or a Zulu there might be some grounds for the predictions of ridicule to be presently incurred by Japan, as well as for the outcry against unnecessary expenditure raised by certain well-meaning but somewhat petulant folk. He happens, however, to be a most agreeable and accomplished gentleman and a dignified one to boot."

The results of the Japanese journey as they bore fruit

for Hawaii were essentially advantageous. Due to the diplomatic gestures of treaty revisions, Hawaii approached Japan for the first time in Japanese foreign relations on equal footing. By recognizing the Imperial Government as an equivalent and respected power, the Hawaiian people won a loyal and indebted foreign ally.

Also resulting from Kalakaua's friendship with the Emperor Meiji was a loosening of royal objections to Japanese immigration to Hawaii. As a power which recognized Japan as an equal, Hawaii was given special consideration in the negotiations taking place between the sugar planter's representatives in Japan and the Imperial Government. In 1884 an agreement was made between Japan and Hawaii which guaranteed the passage, treatment and living conditions of Japanese laborers in Hawaii, and on February 8, 1885 the first major contingent of Japanese immigrants arrived in Honolulu.

Of the other two proposals, the royal marriage and the "Union and Federation of Asiatic nations and sovereigns," no concrete agreements resulted. Japan realized that Kalakaua was not speaking for the American interests in Hawaii. Such a union of Japan and Hawaii might jeopardize the fledgling industrial power which Japan was attempting to develop and the treaty revisions it was seeking. America was still Japan's best friend among foreign powers, and therefore she did not wish to offend the United States in any manner. Thus both the royal marriage and the formation of an Asiatic union were respectively declined in 1882.

To his royal brother in Hawaii the Emperor apologized that he could not take part at that time in the formation of the Asiatic union. "In the face of the internal administration of my government being of such a pressing nature I have not a heart to turn my face from it, and leaving my country, to devote myself mainly to the work which more directly concerns other nations. . . . However, I ardently hope that such Union may be realized at some future day.''

Though the marriage proposal uniting the Imperial and royal courts "deeply moved his heart,'' the Emperor felt that such plans in the face of American interests in Hawaii were premature. Prince Komatsu himself wrote to King Kalakaua to decline the marriage offer. "Through the Reception Committee,'' he wrote, "I was informed of your generous kindness, in asking me, if it would be my happiness to be united to your Royal niece in marriage, I am at a loss to express fully my appreciation of this honor. As I am still under age, I have consulted my father, and I am very reluctantly compelled to decline your distinguished proposal for the reason that I am already betrothed to my future companion in life; so I sincerely trust that your Majesty will not be disappointed at what duty compels me to do.''

Evidently, though, the matter was not put to rest until some years later. Thirteen years after the marriage proposal was made, Princess Kaiulani wrote to her aunt that "I have thought over . . . my marrying some prince from Japan. Unless it is absolutely necessary I would much rather not do so. I could have married an enormously rich German count, but I could not care for him. I feel it would be wrong if I married a man I did not love.''

Though the secret proposals of the evening of March 10, 1881 never reached florescence, one of their consequences was the enhancement of the Japanese-Hawaiian entente in the years of pre-Annexation Hawaii. And perhaps a tribute to the Japanese friendship with the Hawaiian Monarchy was a brief incident on February

23, 1893. When the warship "Naniwa," commanded by Captain Heihachirō Tōgō (later a national hero during the Russo-Japanese War) and with sub-lieutenant Prince Komatsu on board steamed into Honolulu during the turbulent days when the Hawaiian Monarchy was being overthrown, she would not fly the flag of the Republic of Hawaii. Captain Tōgō stubbornly refused to recognize the revolutionary government as legitimate and persuaded other foreign ships to follow suit by declining to salute or hoist the new Hawaiian flag. An infuriated Sanford Dole and various spokesmen began to suspect that the Japanese were intending to invade Hawaii. Responsible organs of public opinion, though, including Japanese residents, insisted that the "Naniwa" was in Honolulu to protect Japanese citizens during the period of unrest. Still, some Hawaiians were so impressed by Tōgō's actions, they supposedly named some of their children "Tōgō" or "Naniwa."

So in many ways, King Kalakaua in his ten days in Japan had achieved much. He created the necessary conditions for an agreement on future Japanese labor which would initiate the waves of immigration which brought the parents of the present day Nisei and Sansei to Hawaii. He formed a diplomatic bond of mutual respect and equality with an Asiatic nation undergoing foreign interference, a bond which twelve years later gave at least moral support to a dying Monarchy and the independence of a Pacific people. He established an atmosphere in Hawaii which saw Japanese immigrants and their children as a welcome part of these Pacific Isles.

Kalakaua's reception in Japan deeply impressed the Hawaiian King. As a result of his visits to various Buddhist temples, he indicated that he was considering introducing Buddhism to Hawaii to enrich the cultural diversity of the Islands. To insure the independence and insularity of the Hawaiiian Monarchy, he was profoundly aroused by the notion of the Japanese Emperor being descended from the sun. Wasn't it possible, Kalakaua reasoned, that the Hawaiian King was descended from the Hawaiian gods or *akuas?*

Feeling close to Japan, when the first group of immigrants arrived from Japan aboard the "City of Tokio" on February 8, 1885, King Kalakaua was at dockside to welcome them to his Kingdom. In his honor, three days later on February 11, the Japanese reciprocated with a sports festival given at the immigration station to which the King, his family and cabinet were invited.

The main event of the day was a *sumo* wrestling match, the first such demonstration in the Hawaiian Islands. Within a large area, an arena was designed by encircling a sandy spot with sand bags in a 12-foot diameter. In the middle of the area was a mound of sand in which a staff decked with streamers of white paper was planted. Near the back of this wrestling ring were ten tubs of what the *Pacific Commercial Advertiser* called "'sahkee,' a favorite Japanese drink." Across the ring on a seat covered with a scarlet blanket were three women playing three-stringed "banjos."

There were 20 wrestlers divided into two teams on opposite sides of the ring. They were naked except for a band of cloth passed between their legs and then wound around their waists. At the signal of the referee two wrestlers, one from each team, jumped into the ring and began to grapple with each other, throwing their opponents to the ground and outside of the ring. As each of the wrestlers entered the arena and fought his oppo-

nent, loud cheers and applause came from the audience
of Japanese.

Except for one brief free-for-all when a small fight
broke out between the wrestlers, the matches progressed
without any disturbing incidents. After one hour, the
referee declared the winning team in a way which puzzled the Hawaiians. "In what mysterious way the question was decided," the *Advertiser* said, "no one outside
of the ring could determine, but all seemed satisfied."

Following the referee's decision the wrestlers com-
menced a slow, stately ring dance fastening around their
waists red, yellow and blue blankets. When they had
finished this brief ceremony, the ten tubs of "sahkee"
were opened and the crowd and royal company in-
dulged in the strange liquor.

Thus ended Hawaii's first *sumo* wrestling match and
taste of *sake* and thus began the sometimes amiable, if
at times somewhat tenuous, history of the people of
Japan living in the Hawaiian Islands. In a foreboding
and ironic sense, the *Advertiser* in describing the *sumo*
matches concluded that "such people on a plantation
would help to make things lively."

It is curious that 88 years after Japan brought *sumo*
wrestling to Hawaii, Hawaii took its special brand of
sumo wrestling back to Japan. Indeed, Jesse Takamiyama Kuhaulua, the "Hawaiian Hero" who in July, 1972
won the Emperor's Cup, the highest prize a *sumo*
wrestler can win, in many ways represents a modern Kalakaua, a restored "Phoenix Fountain" which sym-
bolizes the affinity between Japan and Hawaii. Born on
Maui, a Hawaiian with no Japanese ancestry, Takamiyama struggled through the Japanese training camps
and the years of tournaments to fulfill his ambition of
becoming the first non-Japanese *sumo* wrestler to win

Hawaiian *sumo* wrestler, Jesse Takamiyama Kuhaulua, in Japan. *Photo courtesy of the* Hawaii Hochi.

Japan's most coveted wrestling honor. And as revealed in his recently published autobiography, *Takamiyama: The World of Sumo,* he has also been victorious in bridging the cultures of Hawaii and Japan. "When I am in Hawaii or with American friends in Japan," Jesse writes, "I feel American. And when I'm with other sumotori or Japanese friends, I feel like one of them. It's hard to say which feeling is stronger."

"I will, though, probably settle in Japan after I retire . . . I've lived here since I was nineteen and have gotten very used to the way of life. It would be hard to change back again."

So from Kalakaua and his proposals in Japan, Tōgō

The legacy of friendship and mutual respect between Hawaii and Japan—Princess Kaiulani in kimono. *Photo courtesy of the Hawaii State Archives.*

and the "Naniwa" in Honolulu, the first Issei perform-
ing an exhibition of *sumo* wrestling, to Jesse Takamiyama Kuhaulua, the people of Japan and Hawaii have enjoyed a mutually respectful and rewarding relationship.
The tone set for the treatment of the Japanese in Hawaii
was one of fairness and equality, at least as far as the
Hawaiian plantation and political systems would allow.

Indeed, to comprehend the amiable quality of life in
Hawaii today, the "local" identification and the self-
image of the great majority of Japanese Americans
which represent not the paranoia of an oppressed minority group, but the confidence of a stable and equal
participant in community affairs, the legacy of mutual
respect and friendship between Hawaii and Japan must
be historically understood. In the early days when
Japanese immigrants decided to make Hawaii their
home, they did so because Hawaii could become *home*.

The Japanese Americans today have always considered Hawaii as the land to which they belong. Only by
appreciating the initial character of Japan-Hawaii relations, the friendliness accorded the Japanese in the past
on the personal, day-to-day level, can we understand
why so many Issei, Nisei and Sansei show such a loyal
and endearing attachment to the Hawaiian Islands.
Only then can we understand why over 50 years ago the
Japanese would erect a fountain to show everlasting importance to the equality and friendship between the
people of Hawaii and Japan.

But to paint too pleasant a picture of the past is not a
totally responsible accomplishment in the face of other
less accommodating factors. To be sure, the Japanese
like all of Hawaii's people have in Hawaii a home they
love. They treat each other in most cases openly and
equally. Yet part of the identity which the Japanese

American has inherited from the past is an animosity and racial deference transmitted through the social conditions and practices which the plantation system patterned and bred. It is an historic message which still affects the relations of the races in Hawaii and which must be recognized as the legacy of prejudice—a legacy of racial uneasiness with which all of the people of Hawaii must still deal.

6
Reaping the Whirlwind

Eight o'clock in the morning to most youngsters always seems too dreadfully early, especially when that is the time school starts. But young Gill Jamieson on that Tuesday morning of September 18, 1928, wasn't overly concerned with having to interrupt his sleep to go to classes. He was an exceptionally bright and enthusiastic student who actually looked forward to his days spent at Punahou, the private school for children of the most exclusive families.

Going to school in Hawaii in 1928 was still the casual affair it had always been. Gill put on his flannel knee-pants and wore a light-colored sport shirt; he didn't bother to wear any shoes. After all, Gill knew that sitting in those small classrooms on a hot and humid September afternoon caused the body to become sweaty and sticky.

Gill's father, Frederick Jamieson, called from the kitchen that Gill had better hurry or they would be late. Every morning on his way to his office at the Hawaiian Trust Company where he was vice-president, Frederick would drop his son, his only child, off at school.

As they left their home at 2751 Kahawai Street and drove down the valley to Punahou, a light rain and rainbow filled the Manoa sky. It was going to be a typically beautiful day in Honolulu, and didn't a light rain signify good luck according to old Hawaiian legends? Driving into the school through the main entrance on the corner of Wilder and Punahou Streets, Frederick left his son at the front of the elementary classrooms and then drove on to his downtown office.

The morning routine at Punahou wasn't much different that day from any other day—the same lessons, exercises and reprimands. But on this Tuesday the time for mid-morning recess had been changed. Instead of going onto the playground for 15 minutes of eating, joking and horseplay at 9:45 as they had always done, this morning the students had their recess at 9:30.

During recess as Gill played with his classmates, anyone could have distinguished him from the others. He was fairly tall for his age of ten years, and was therefore a dominant figure among the other elementary school children. He stood four feet nine and one-half inches and had an unusually erect carriage. His blue eyes and light brown hair combed over his forehead gave him that boyishly handsome appearance which characterized his distinguished haole family.

As recess ended, Gill was unexpectedly called to the attendance office. "What is the trouble?" he thought anxiously. Had he done something wrong? When he entered the office, he was approached by Miss Mary Winne, the elementary principal.

"Gill, your mother has been injured in an automobile accident. We don't know how she is, but I am sure everything will be alright. Someone from the hospital is going to be coming to pick you up any moment now."

GILL JAMIESON

Gill Jamieson. *Reprinted from the* Honolulu Star-Bulletin.

His mother involved in a car accident? Was she badly hurt? Was she dying? These thoughts rushed through his mind as he raced out of the attendance office to the school library. "I should have something to read to my mother," he thought, "especially if she is going to be in bed for a long time." He chose a short story which was one of his favorites, *Father's Gone A-Whaling*, and returned to nervously wait for the car which would take him to his injured mother's side.

On the last day of his peaceful and unnoticed life, a life spent in mediocrity and anonymity, Myles Yutaka Fukunaga awoke in his rented hotel room at 5:30 A.M., anxious that this was the day for which he had long awaited. As was to be his daily practice every morning for nearly a week, Myles began the day by reading the *Honolulu Advertiser* and *Star-Bulletin*. He searched for news about the kidnapper-murderer William Hickman of Los Angeles. Had he been executed yet? He read about a new series of mainland murderers, the so-called "club murders" where the victims' heads were found brutally battered. And in the tradition of the most avid newspaper readers in the twenties, he read the first installment of a new novel by Eleanor Early, *The Whirlwind*, serialized in the *Star-Bulletin*. "They have sown the wind," the biblical quotation from *Hosea* read, "and they shall reap the whirlwind."

At eight o'clock this small and seemingly frail boy of 19 years left his room at the Serene Hotel, a room which he had rented that previous Saturday, and went to a small cafe where he ordered breakfast. But he was too nervous to eat, and could only consume a small portion of the meal.

Myles then searched out a telephone in a small shop

Miles Yutaka Fukunaga, confessed slayer and kidnapper of Gill is picture of him was taken following his confession early this even

IEN WHO FIGURE IN CAPTURE OF FUKUN

Myles Fukunaga. *Reprinted from the* Honolulu Star-Bulletin.

on Beretania Street near Smith Street which was operated by an elderly Japanese lady. He first called Mrs. Frederick Jamieson, saying that he was a member of the board of health. "How many children do you have Mrs. Jamieson?" he inquired.

"One," she answered.

Then he called the Hawaiian Trust Co. to ask whether a Mr. Jamieson worked at the establishment. "Yes," he was told. Finally he called Punahou School and talked to Miss Jean Winne, the chief registrar.

"Do you have in your school the son of F. W. Jamieson?"

She couldn't understand the question which was asked in a heavily accented voice which sounded like German or French. She asked the caller to wait, she would get the principal, her sister Mary. Unable to locate Mary, she had to take the call herself. The caller repeated the question more clearly.

"I don't know; we have some Jamieson boys in school," Miss Winne answered. "Is it Gordon or Billy you mean?" Gordon and Billy were Gill's cousins.

"The mother says she has only one boy. He is ten years old."

"Oh, you must mean Gill. What's wrong?"

"The boy's mother has been hurt in an automobile accident. We will send a hospital orderly to pick him up immediately."

"How is Mrs. Jamieson?" Miss Winne inquired.

The voice was hesitant, uncertain. "I am sorry, but I cannot tell you that. You'll have to talk to the doctor."

After Myles had finished his phone call, he went to a taxi-cab stand and hired a brown Packard driven by M. Yoshioka. Myles was wearing a white jacket and pants so as to resemble a hospital orderly and wore dark glasses to disguise his face. He spoke in fluent Japanese to Yoshioka, who drove Myles to Punahou School. As they drove onto the school grounds at 10:00, the children were already back in their classes after recess, so none of them saw the car, its license or Myles.

When Myles entered the attendance office he met Miss Mary Winne, who by then had been informed of the emergency. As they waited for Gill to return from the library, she looked carefully into his face. "There was nothing sophisticated or tricky about the face," she was to say later. "It was a nice face with regular features. Although he had on dark glasses, I could see his eyes plainly and they looked directly at me without flickering."

When Gill arrived, Myles led him to the waiting taxi and they both got into the back seat. The Packard maneuvered a turnabout and exited through the main entrance of the school at Punahou and Wilder Streets. As they drove through the streets of Moiliili, heading towards Kalakaua Ave. and Waikiki, Myles tried to converse with Gill. At the same time, he began to make a strained and anguished decision. The young boy seemed pleasant enough; he was actually very cute. Should Myles kill him?

Gill ignored Myles' advances of friendship. He was concerned with his mother's condition and could think of little else. And yet this strange hospital attendant could only quiz him. "I asked the boy all kinds of questions," Myles was to say, "only he answered me yes and yes. . . . Purposely I bought some candy and gave him. He didn't eat the candy." Myles' decision was made.

The taxi stopped at the entrance of the Royal Hawaiian Hotel where the passengers disembarked. Gill became nervous and apparently frightened; this wasn't the hospital! Myles reassured him that this is where the automobile accident occured; his mother was waiting for him. They crossed Kalakaua Avenue and entered the grounds of the Seaside Hotel, Myles telling Gill that this was a short cut. In the rear of the Seaside cottages, near the Ala Wai canal, Myles led Gill through a dense thicket of *kiawe* and overgrowth.

Here Myles had prepared weeks previously a "den," a hollowed out place in the ground beneath a palm tree, fenced in on all sides by *kiawe* trees. At 11:15, nearly one hour after the abduction, Myles struck Gill on the head with a tempered steel chisel, blood splattering Myles' clean white jacket and trousers. The boy screamed and began to struggle. Again a blow from the chisel landed on the boy's head. The lad was stronger than Myles had estimated, and the air in the compact enclosure was filled with the terrifying screams of the youngster trying to save himself. Finally, a third blow from the chisel rendered the victim senseless. After the body fell to the ground, Myles wrapped his hands around the tiny throat and squeezed out the last breaths of Gill's life.

What makes a man commit murder, especially the murder of a ten-year-old boy for no apparent reason, is a question we laymen leave for police, criminologists, psychologists, lawyers and novelists. What logic or illogic is employed, what twisted or macabre drives are required, are unimaginable and unintelligible to the "sane" individual. Only the brutality of an inhuman monster, we conclude, could split open the skull of a harmless child.

To those who knew him, Myles Fukunaga was not a monster, an insensitive brute. To the contrary, exceptionally bright, a good student with a pleasing personality and gentle nature, Myles was a clean-cut Nisei youth who seemingly had had a very typical upbringing. Born February 4, 1909, in Makaweli, Kauai, Myles was the son of a Japanese plantation worker. He attended Eleele and Kapaa schools, achieving an excellent record, until his family moved to Waialua, Oahu, in December of 1924. On Oahu he graduated from Waialua Grammar School at the head of his class. During the summer he worked in the pineapple fields and when his family moved to Honolulu, both he and his father worked at the Queen's Hospital. In March 1928 he was hospitalized for appendicitis causing him to lose his hospital job. In June, when he had recovered, he found employment at the Seaside Hotel.

At the Seaside, Myles gained a good reputation, as he had gained everywhere else. The head-waiter at the hotel said that he had never known a boy quite like Myles. "Ordinary boys could not be trusted, but Myles was different. Myles was trustworthy, smiling, clean and never 'saucy.'"

But Myles was also considered to be too moody, thoughtful and reserved. He had been hungry for an education, but his family, living in a small house near the corner of Beretania and Alapai Streets, needed the income which he as the eldest son of six children could provide. Robbed of his education, needing to work at jobs which paid him $40 a month, $35 of which he would give his mother, Myles turned to reading and daydreaming to fill his boring days. He would memorize passages from Shakespeare or various verses of poetry which he would occasionally recite when he spoke. Lonely, with no close friends or female companionship, he began to retreat into a world of his own making where his life took on meaning and this small, barely five-feet-tall Japanese boy could become noticed and respected.

In March of 1928 before he was hospitalized at Queen's for appendicitis, Myles had attempted suicide but failed miserably. But what was worse, by his actions he had shamed his parents and he felt a need to achieve honor, thus redeeming himself in their eyes. He must do something to help them out of their state of abject poverty. He must earn enough money to send his parents back to Japan where they so earnestly desired to go.

The plans to commit a crime to earn the money became more intense in May. As he was at home recuperating from his illness of March, his mother was visited by a man from the Hawaiian Trust Co. who came to collect the rent on the house. The mother asked the agent if he could wait a month, since her son was still an invalid. But in June, she pleaded, Myles would be able to go back to work in the pineapple fields.

According to the story which Myles was later to tell, the agent said, "no, you'll have to pay this rent immediately." The mother could pay only $40 of the $45 rent, exhausting her small supply of money. She went into her bedroom after the Hawaiian Trust man left and began to sob incessantly. Myles, in the next room, overheard.

Again, because he had been ill, he had failed his parents. Again he felt they were shamed because of their son's inability to support them. The plans for revenge against Hawaiian Trust and at the same time to earn money for his parents' return to Japan began to be formulated.

Daily he visited the State library reading everything he could about the Leopold and Loeb kidnapping-murder case on the mainland in the early twenties, as well as the recent Hickman case in Los Angeles. He copied their plans out of a bizarre desire to emulate Americans. Throughout his life Myles had been driven by a desire to be accepted as an American, and now he chose to commit a horrendous crime in the best American tradition. He made maps of Manoa Valley, penciling in the home of his intended victim, Frederick Jamieson. Myles felt that Jamieson was the wealthiest executive of Hawaiian Trust who had a son that could be kidnapped. He then moved out of his parents' home on Beretania and Alapai and rented a room in the Serene Hotel in downtown Honolulu.

At the Seaside Hotel, he became remote from his fellow employees. He started to spend his time in the "den" near the Ala Wai where the kidnapping and murder plans became detailed. To make sure that the other employees wouldn't find out about his scheme, he would strategically place magazines in the "den" while he was gone. If he ever found them moved, he reasoned, someone was invading his hideout. The magazines were never disturbed.

So as September 18 neared, a date marked on his calendar, this lonely, socially rejected boy began to anticipate the events of the coming week. He would, by his actions, bring honor to his parents by being able to send them home to Japan. He would win his revenge against the Hawaiian Trust for its ill-treatment of his family. He would show that he was as intelligent and as deadly an American as the very best. He would prove himself a man worth reckoning with by a dramatic and powerful act. He confided in no one, so no one could bring rationality to his plans. His world was composed of paper and ink with little human contact, so he had no deep feeling of humanity which could restrain him. In his mind a thousand influencing and yet conflicting patterns led him into his actions so that no moral consciousness or guilt could hamper him. As the hands of Myles Fukunaga ended the life of Gill Jamieson, they felt no hesitation, no remorse; the play which Myles was acting out was reaching its startling climax which would shake Honolulu and the Japanese American community to their very foundations.

Mary and Jean Winne had not noticed the car which supposedly took their student Gill Jamieson to the hospital. It was not unusual for chauffeurs to pick up the students of Punahou, so they felt no special need to verify the authenticity of the accident or the hospital orderly.

Several hours later Mary Winne called the Jamieson home to inquire about the condition of Mrs. Jamieson. To her astonishment she was told by Mrs. Jamieson herself that there had been no automobile accident, no injury. "But we received a telephone call this morning that there had been an accident. We released Gill to the custody of a hospital orderly." Something, Mrs. Jamieson realized, was horribly wrong.

At about the same time, 1:30, a 15-year-old Filipino messenger from the Territorial Messenger Service, Alfred Reyes, delivered a letter which he had received from a Japanese youth at the Nuuanu Y.M.C.A. addressed to Frederick Jamieson, Hawaiian Trust. The letter was written on two sheets of white stationery in ink. The handwriting style was clearly legible in a manner which "experts" testified as typical of the "oriental hand."

K   K   K
Will God Save the Kings?

Tuesday Sept. 18
This day no other
9 A.M.

Mr. Frederick W. Jamieson, Esq.

Sir:

The Fates have decided so we have been given this privilege in writing you on this important matter. We presume you will be alarmed at first. Nevertheless, we hope that you get over this surprise soon and listen to the writer's story. What is it all about?

YOUR SON IS KIDNAPPED FOR RANSOM.

Let us be calm in this. We assure you that your son is at present well and safe. He will be as long as you obey each and every one of our commands. If on the other hand you do not carry out our instructions, you can hope for nothing but Death to your son. We mean it.

Sir,

In your business life, you no doubt have found that "Confidence" in your fellowman is a great factor. Isn't that true? Now, here in this case, we want you to have utmost confidence in us. Have all fears swept aside. Do what we say and you will see your son again. Fight us, and you will never see him, nay he will be but a shadow; lifeless. But let us not dwell on the tragedy. Make your decision on the better side of it. Below are the instructions on which the whole matter depends.

YOU ARE TO CARRY OUT THE FOLLOWING

I. Keep this matter a Secret. Do not notify or seek help from outside, i.e. police or detectives. (Let us remind you this—that every kidnapping case we have studied,

"Will God Save the Kings?" *Reprinted from the* Honolulu Star-Bulletin.

"outsiders" have been notified and all with disastrous results on both parties. Do you want this to happen? We advise you that any trickery be avoided. As we say; have confidence and cooperate with us).

II. Have ten thousand dollars (10,000) on hand today before 2 P.M. They are to be entirely of Old Bills of the following denomination:—

$4,000 in ten dollar and five dollar bills
$4,000 in twenty dollars bills
$2,000 in fifty dollar bills

$10,000—total amount—no more notes

Now then—these must be free of any identification whatsoever. Any attempt to mark or take numbers or any attempt to trace the money will render the entire venture futile.

III. Have money in plain wrapper securely. Also have all letters addressed to you by us wrapped together with the bills. Do not destroy letters. Simply return them by that method. Do not take samples of the writing though we have no fear. We are too cautious—even the "telltale" typewriter is not used by us. Remember we know our business as you know yours thoroughly. Nothing will prevent us from seeking our ultimate goal.

IV. This is the manner in which we are to meet and exchange our holdings. The time and place is to be given you later by phone or letter. Be prepared for it. Come alone prepared with car to (?) time (?) place. Stop at directed place, lights out 10 seconds then on. Await. First man will come to you there. Let him enter the car. His purpose is to see who you are and to see that there is no foul play. Another purpose is to see if you have the right amount of money on hand. Show and count for him. If all is well he will tell you to blow the horn, a signal for the rest of us to approach you with your son in another car. Transaction to be made then and there before your eyes. Be true and so be it.

V. Obey all further instructions when given to you by phone or letter. Be at home at 9 o'clock P.M. when we either telephone or send you a letter directing when and where to come for the meeting.

Sir,

The world is a mere stage in which we humans are the humble actors or players. We are about to play our part in our secret drama entitled "THE THREE VANISH-INK SHADOWS." Note that we are but three poor walking shadows.

Right on your receipt of this letter, you are to be watched by us, your action and your every detailed movement. So beware. You are not dealing with a lone hand. We want to make it simple for you. Just do as we have instructed and all be well with all. We want clean money unspotted by blood. But any false move on your part will result in death.

It comes to this—we are placing your son's life on your own shoulders. And then ours will be at stake too.

Who knows, perhaps, yours too, even. Then yours will be the decision to decide our fate. A lot of responsibility for one. Be true and you will not regret it. What is money compared to life, sir: We know all will come out the way we want. We trust you.

As a final warning—this is a strictly commercial proposition and we are prepared to put our threat into execution should we have reasonable grounds to believe that you have committed an infraction of the above instructions. However should you carefully carry out our commands faithfully, we can assure you that your son will be safely returned to you right on the minute that we make our prearranged transactions.

Do right by us and we will do the same. Do wrong and we will stop at nothing. Too much words have been wasted but we hope this long letter will get you thinking straight. After all "THE THREE SHADOWS" will walk to an end. So let us do our best as planned. We hope you will like our "directorship."

End of "Three Walking Shadows"
End of "Three Walking Shadows"
"Never was a kingdom so poor
    or foolish X   X   X
    We 3 "KINGS"
    without crowns
        The Three Kings

K x K x K x

Perpendicularly down the first sheet was printed "its no joke, read carefully, think wise, don't delay." The second sheet bore the quotation emphasized by three crudely drawn crosses: "Oh Father forgive them they know not what they do."

Immediately the frantic father phoned his home. Yes, he learned, Gill had been mysteriously abducted from school by a Japanese male in white clothing and dark glasses. Then Frederick Jamieson called the McDuffie International Detective Agency to employ Arthur Mc-Duffie to find his son. In compliance with the letter's instruction for secrecy, the police were not informed.

News of the kidnapping and ransom letter, however, could hardly be confined in the close-knit community of Manoa Valley where fearful husbands and fathers were soon organizing search teams to scan the area. The police were informed of the kidnapping but at the vigorous insistence of Jamieson, all overt activity was ceased.

The long afternoon and evening of waiting ended at 8:41 when the telephone rang in the Jamieson home. Gill's father answered the phone and heard a voice tell him to go immediately to Thomas Square at the corner of Beretania and Ward Streets and then follow the instructions in the letter. Those standing near the phone could only hear Jamieson's trembling voice over the heavy rain on the roof and the barking of the neighbor's dog.

"Where's my boy?" they heard him ask. "Is he there with you? Let me talk to him."

Finally they heard him answering, "He is worth more than that to me. At 9 o'clock? I'll be there."

Jamieson was followed to Thomas Square by two carloads of police detectives crammed into the automobiles. But there was a mishap, and Jamieson arrived fifteen minutes before the detectives. He parked his car on Beretania, across the street from the Honolulu Academy of Arts on the mauka side of Thomas Square facing Waikiki. Following instructions he blinked his headlights several times.

From the darkness a man appeared with a handkerchief shielding his eyes and carrying a concealed hammer. He got into the car and ordered Jamieson to drive down Beretania to Victoria, down Victoria to King and toward Waikiki on King Street to a dirt road near McKinley High School baseball field where he was told to park.

Jamieson was then told by the masked passenger to remove his hat and count the ransom money into it. As he was counting out the money, the man began to raise a hammer as if to strike Jamieson.

"You had better not try anything," Jamieson warned sharply. The man dropped the weapon and became visibly shaken.

"That's enough money," he demanded after only $4,000 had been counted out. "I'll get the boy." He then scurried out of the car and into the grounds of

McKinley High School. But the kidnapper with Gill never reappeared. Confused as to what was supposed to happen, Jamieson returned to his office to wait for word of his son. Evidently something had gone awry and the fate of the young Jamieson boy hung on the whimsy of the three kidnappers who had so boldly defied the social calm of Hawaii.

In very short order, the secret of the Jamieson boy's kidnapping became terrifying news to the populace of Honolulu. The *Honolulu Star-Bulletin* ran a special edition which hit the streets at 11:00 P.M. with photographs of Gill and a list of the serial numbers of the ransom money so as to aid those who sought the boy and the Three Kings.

Honolulu had witnessed horrible crimes before, but not on the scale of the paranoia which accompanied the Jamieson kidnapping. The racial status quo which predicated the establishment of the oligarchy and so tightly structured pre-World War II Hawaii was threatened by so brash an action as the abduction of a haole boy whose father was vice-president of a major economic power. The Three Kings became a symbol of terror very quickly as the population of Honolulu poured into the downtown quarters to wait for news of the boy, the Three Kings and the Japanese suspects in the case. Rumors flew that other haole families could expect the same tragedy, that so-and-so's son had been murdered, that such-and-such a suspect had been arrested.

The police force was sadly ill-prepared to deal with a crime of this proportion. The Three Kings were obviously only part of a larger crime wave, and very few clues were offered the police. What was needed, the authorities deduced, was an extensive house-to-house search of Honolulu. To accomplish this, organizations were asked to enlist members to join in the search. Private citizens were deputized at the National Armory Headquarters downtown, and posses were formed to search homes, backyards, valleys and vacant lots in hopes of finding clues, suspects or the boy.

Among the groups which joined in the search beginning Wednesday morning September 19 were the McKinley Boy Scouts, 20,000 school children released from school and led by ROTC cadets from Punahou and Kamehameha Schools, the American Legion and every civilian group in Honolulu. The Army and Navy joined the search and in the sky a single available airplane scanned Oahu from Waianae to Makapuu. The boy and the Three Kings must be found; the talk in the streets turned to lynching. Hawaii had never before had a case of lynching, but never before had a haole boy been kidnapped.

As Wednesday evening enveloped the town, there was no news of the boy or the Three Kings. In desperation, some leaders in the community felt that the civil authorities were too impotent, too amateurish. At Pier 2 that evening a group calling themselves the Vigilante Corps and chaired by John A. Balch, discussed what actions were needed to arrest the culprits and recover the boy. What new laws governing kidnapping and public execution, they demanded, were needed to instill the necessary fear in those who might think of kidnapping a haole child again?

In every sense, Honolulu was becoming an armed camp of roaming posses and fearful, excited men, women and children. One could not travel the streets without having to pass roadblocks set up at major intersections such as Puuloa Road and Kamehameha Highway and Nuuanu and Wyllie Streets. The police station was inundated with calls reporting possible clues and suspects. A woman in Kaimuki heard a child screaming at night; a man in Waimanalo heard a strange man shouting "Have you a boy in there?" The Japanese ex-chauffeur of the Jamieson family, Harry Kaisan, was arrested as possibly one of the Three Kings. He was detained, questioned and he allegedly confessed to writing the ransom note after being injected with hyoscine hydrobromide or "truth serum." When the drug wore off, the frightened and anxious suspect repudiated his confession; he had spent the day, he insisted, playing poker at a pool hall.

Thursday morning at approximately 8:30 the *Star-Bulletin* received a cryptic letter from the Three Kings, verified by the enclosure of a $5 bill, identified as being part of the ransom money.

To Whom it May Concern,

As a result of our recent exploits, we "Three Kings" find the community all agog and in a state of suspense and terror for the lost lad. To relieve it we have decided to clear just a part of the mystery.

Mas. Gill Jamieson, poor innocent lad, has departed for the Unknown, a forlorn "Walking Shadow" in the Great Beyond, where we all go to when the time comes.

Circumstances prevent us from giving full information in regard to the body's whereabouts. As to ours, we'll leave the many detectives to apprehend us. When the "pests" fail to do that, we will, as God's in Heaven, reveal ourselves to the light of justice. When? Life is short when thoughts of leaving it forever comes to you. The day shall be on the 25th, exactly a week after the crime had been committed when we promise to mount on the scaffold of sin to plead guilty and the death penalty we are to receive.

Meanwhile we hope that God will watch over us as he had done during our adventures in crime. We are bad,

bad and we'll let Him decide whether we shall be caught before hand. We will not complain but accept his wishes as they befall on us.

The wrong cannot be righted now. We only regret that we have brought sorrows to the parents of the boy and ours and to the community in general.

The worst of fears had been confirmed; the Jamieson boy had no doubt been murdered. The hysteria in Honolulu reached a new fervor as the *Advertiser* reflected in an editorial which called for revenge. "Make the penalty death," the newspaper demanded. More Japanese suspects in addition to Harry Kaisan were arrested. Kazue Nakamura, who protested that he knew nothing about the case, was arrested after he was identified as the man who gave Alfred Reyes the letter in the Nuuanu Y.M.C.A. When he faced Nakamura, Alfred began shouting, "That's him! I know that's him! Look at him . . . same nose . . . same shirt." Police were convinced Nakamura had to be involved with the Three Kings because in his room they found what appeared to be a battle plan for an attack on Pearl Harbor. "I was only day dreaming, make-believing," Nakamura insisted. "I know nothing about the kidnapping."

A Japanese boy mailing a letter at the Waikiki Tavern was arrested as a possible suspect even though he pleaded that the police officers should read the innocent letter. Two young Japanese calling on a friend who worked at the home of a wealthy haole were chased by a watchman; one of them was caught and arrested. What had they, Japanese, been doing approaching a haole's home? Indeed, as the city continued to search for the boy's body, all eyes turned on the Japanese community to see what they were doing to help in the Jamieson case.

The *Star-Bulletin* and Mayor of Honolulu Charles Arnold gave good reasons for insisting throughout Wednesday and Thursday of September 19 and 20 that the Jamieson kidnapping was not a racial crime. Even though the Three Kings were most likely Japanese, and Japanese were the primary suspects who were being arrested, making the Jamieson case into a racial issue was too dangerous for the precarious balance of Hawaii's racial structure. The kidnapping was already becoming the instigation for possible race riots and bloodshed as Honolulu very literally became hysterical. The situation demanded tight control over the rampant forces of racial hostility so that despite the threatening situation, the illusion of racial tranquility and harmony could be maintained.

Needless to say, on the street level, the Japanese community as a whole was being blamed for the crime. The Three Kings were Japanese and their actions seemed an expression of racial revenge, hatred or jealousy. In every sense of the word, the Japanese community would have to prove itself innocent by concerted and tireless efforts to join with Hawaii's other races to apprehend the criminals. As the *Nippu Jiji* stated, "In case the kidnappers were definitely identified to be Japanese, it would mean a dirty stain on the escutcheon of the Japanese in the islands."

When the news of the kidnapping first was announced, one of the first groups to volunteer in the search was the Japanese Taxi-Cab Drivers Association which provided automobiles and manpower. Japanese volunteered in the search; Japanese donated to a collection taken by the Honolulu Chamber of Commerce to provide a reward to persons helping in the apprehension of the Three Kings; the Japanese Students' Alliance in Hilo sent condolences to the Jamieson family; the

Japanese Consul General profusely apologized to the people of Honolulu on behalf of the Japanese race; the Japanese Chamber of Commerce announced that "being the duty of every citizen and resident of the Territory of Hawaii to rise to this occasion, it is urged that every Japanese resident cooperate and strive to locate the missing boy, Gill Jamieson."

One of the most active searchers was Fred Makino, editor of the *Hawaii Hochi*. Working from his office, receiving clues and going out into the streets, Makino recognized that the Japanese community, to show its disinvolvement with the crime and to destroy the image that the crime was racially instigated, should take the lead in the pursuit of the criminals. In fact, Makino had clues that the Three Kings were not Japanese at all; they were Filipinos. As the haole community searched the Japanese district, Makino was patrolling the Filipino residential areas looking for suspects.

The *Hochi* stated, "they had cooperated in every way possible in the effort to locate the Jamieson boy, and in subsequent drives to discover the guilty parties. The entire Japanese community is eager to aid in any way in its power to apprehend the criminals."

The Japanese were so anxious to prosecute the guilty parties that when Harry Kaisan, the Japanese ex-chauffeur, was finally released as not being involved in the crime, he demanded police protection. He felt he needed to be in police custody because the Japanese community was incensed against him. Until his innocence could be clearly proven and things calmed down, he wished to stay in Oahu prison, living in the guard's cottages.

The uncertainty of Gill Jamieson's fate upon which the reputation and even survival of the Japanese community in Hawaii depended, was ended at 11:15 A.M. Thursday morning by Carl Vickery. The young man, part of a search team, found the body of the missing ten-year-old boy in a small glade near the Ala Wai canal opposite the Royal Hawaiian Hotel. The body was found neatly laid on a mat of old gunny sacks. The chest and face were covered with old issues of the *American Weekly* newspaper, over which lay three palm fronds. The boy was still clothed in the same shirt and trousers he had worn that Tuesday morning. A crude cross made from sticks and tied together by white string was placed over the body.

In the boy's outstretched left hand was a rough copy of a poem, "Immortality" by Spencer McGann, which in part read "There is no death/The wind of yesterday, nothing shall die/The rose that bloomed last May/Will wake next spring as sweet and subtly fair."

On a piece of cardboard was scrawled the following message:

"If you want to die, have you the right to kill others so that you in turn will be killed?"

"It is for you to decide."

"Tomorrow, and tomorrow and tomorrow."

"Creps (creeps) this petty pace from day to day and all our yesterdays—fools the way to dust death-out, and brief candle, life is just a mere shadow—a poor player that frets and struts his hours upon the stage and then is heard no more—It is a tale told by a idiot, flesh of sound and fury signifying nothing. Three Kings. KKK."

Between young Gill's legs, the Three Kings had placed *Father's Gone A-Whaling,* the book which Gill had rushed to the library to get before the hospital attendant came to take him to his mother's side.

Myles sat beside the boy's body for nearly a half hour and wept. Here he had committed a violent act to prove his manhood, and he couldn't even kill a ten-year-old boy correctly. There had been too much of a struggle; he hadn't subdued his victim quickly and efficiently.

For the first time in his life he began to smoke a cigar. He had heard that smoking was relaxing to the nerves, and his trembling body needed something soothing. Anyway, by leaving a cigar near the body the police would be looking for an older man. As he sat near Gill, smoking and weeping, he wrote a verse from *MacBeth* on cardboard and put it over the boy's face. He covered the body with newspapers and palm leaves and stuffed into its left hand a quickly written poem. Nearby he found a crudely constructed Christian cross. How fitting, he thought, as he placed it over the body. He then cut the tops off three playing cards, all Kings, and strew the symbolic clues of the Three Kings around the area. The police, he reasoned, would think that a gang of three murderers, Three Kings, had committed the foul deed.

After disposing of his blood-soaked clothes in the Seaside servants' quarters, Myles boarded a streetcar on Kalakaua and got off downtown near the post office. There he bought a stamped envelope into which he placed his carefully worded ransom letter. He had intended to go into the Hawaiian Trust Company and hand the letter to Frederick Jamieson himself, but he became frightened at the last moment. So he went to the Nuuanu Y.M.C.A. and telephoned for a messenger boy. When Alfred Reyes appeared and demanded 35¢ to deliver the letter, Myles had to go to a nearby store to cash a dollar bill. He bought a package of chewing gum, but he was so nervous he dropped his change all over the floor.

The ransom letter delivered, Myles returned to the Serene Hotel where he waited until 8:00. As he sat in his dingy room all he could hear were the screams of the Jamieson boy. "What have I done?" he asked himself. But the drama must continue; the world is a stage and he is merely a shadow. After 8 o'clock he began to choose a location for the delivery of the money. First he went to Iolani Palace, but no, there were too many police and lights. Besides, the National Guardsmen were drilling nearby. So he chose as an alternative spot, Thomas Square, where at 8:45 he instructed Frederick Jamieson to go.

Whether Myles had actually intended to kill Frederick Jamieson as a part of his elaborate but warped plans, no one can say. When he raised the hammer to strike and Jamieson confronted him, Myles was intimidated and lost his nerve. Not realizing that he had only $4,000 of the ransom money, he fled from the car. He climbed over a wire fence into McKinley's baseball field, cutting his arm on the barbed wire. Crossing Piikoi and King Streets, Myles jumped over another fence and hid behind a hibiscus hedge while automobiles passed. Making his way to Keeaumoku Street by way of backyards and side-streets, Myles hired a taxi which returned him to the Serene Hotel around 10:30.

But Myles couldn't sleep or eat. His mind kept dwelling on the crime he had committed. The boy's face and screams haunted him. Not only that, he had been a coward that day. He must prove to himself that he was still a man.

As Honolulu reached a peak of turmoil and armed posses began their house-to-house searches, Myles left his room Wednesday morning and went straight to the National Guard Armory. He asked if he could be deputized so as to aid in the search of the Three Kings.

"Sorry," he was told. "You're too young and small. You're just a boy."

The suspense and activity he had caused thrilled Myles, but when he read in the newspapers about what he had done, he became bitterly remorseful. He sent a letter to the *Star-Bulletin* announcing that the boy was dead and that the criminals would give themselves up on September 25th, one week after the crime. After all, he had always intended to pay with his life for the crime after his parents had the money to go to Japan.

On Friday Gill Jamieson was buried in the Nuuanu cemetery at a ceremony attended by hundreds. Telegrams from capitals around the world came into Honolulu with condolences for the Jamieson family. A small wreath of flowers was delivered to the burial site with a card signed, "The Three Kings."

After he purchased the flowers for the Jamieson boy Myles went to the main depot of the Oahu Railway and Land Co. and purchased a one-way ticket to Waialua. For reasons only known to Myles, he left Honolulu Saturday morning. Perhaps he wanted to see his old neighborhood and school before he was caught. Perhaps he was trying to elude the tight network of searchers in Honolulu. Perhaps he was trying to escape the screams of Gill Jamieson.

At any rate, Saturday Myles spent walking the streets of Waialua, visiting the *okazu* stand at Yamada's store. But still Myles couldn't eat. He bought a return ticket to Honolulu with one of the ransom bills and complained to the ticket agent that news of the Jamieson case was slow getting to Waialua. "Why can't you get the newspapers out here quicker?" he demanded.

The ticket agent quickly recognized the bill which Myles gave him from the list of serial numbers published in the *Star-Bulletin*. Since Myles was known in Waialua, the police in Honolulu were immediately informed that it was possible that young Fukunaga was one of the Three Kings.

With this information, police visited the Fukunaga home at Beretania and Alapai Streets and searched Myles' room. The maps of Manoa were found as well as other evidence referring to the Three Kings. Tomorrow, his 12-year-old sister promised, she would help the police find her brother.

The last evening of his freedom, Myles played poker with the other tenants of the Serene Hotel, an unprecedented gesture; he had usually ignored everyone. As they played cards, Henry Sato began to talk about the Jamieson case and how he'd like to wring the necks of the Three Kings. "Whoever did the dirty trick," Myles added, "surely had a hell of a lotta nerve."

Sunday morning Myles awoke and donned a clean blue shirt and neatly placed gray tie. He slicked back his hair in a pompadour style and went downtown to watch some movies, one of his favorite pastimes. First he went to the Empire Theater and saw Tim McCoy, America's favorite cowboy, in "Riders in the Dark." Then he saw a light comedy and musical, "Ship Ahoy" at the State Theater. Following this entertainment he walked down Fort Street and stood in front of the Catholic Church watching the Sunday crowds walk by. Suddenly, he noticed his sister with three large haole men walking toward him. His adventures, he instinctively knew, were coming to an anticlimatic end.

"Is your name Fukunaga?" they demanded.

"Yes, that's my name."

"Did you kill the boy?"

"Yes," was his direct answer.

The detectives grabbed Myles by the wrist and began to drag him into their car. "Let go my wrists," he protested. "I won't break away. I'll get into the car."

On the ride to the police station the shrill sound of the siren from Aloha Tower was heard. The siren was intended to signal the National Guard to prevent possible riots, but its effect was to signal the populace of Honolulu that the Three Kings had been caught. Crowds rushed into the downtown area and jammed the streets to look at the killers, jeer them and demand their deaths. No doubt many were surprised to see in the back seat of the car a young, innocent looking Japanese boy, neatly dressed and attired with a tie.

"Will you confess?" the detectives asked Myles as they drove throught the crowds. "Yes, I'll tell you the whole story."

As he was taken out of the car, the crowd pushed nearer. "Look out," one of the police called, "don't let the mob get him."

"Let them get me!" shouted Myles. "I guess I deserve it. I'm not afraid."

Fire engines were called out to clear the angry crowds with the stinging spray of pressurized water. The mayor and police chief both made public statements to the mob that the killer had been apprehended. The Three Kings had merely been a ruse to throw the police off the killer's trail. Myles Fukunaga had made a complete and detailed confession of the crime, so everyone should please go home.

"I am a bad, bad boy," Myles sobbed to the police, and no doubt both his parents and the Japanese community wholeheartedly agreed. But how could such a nice looking, intelligent young man commit such a heinous crime? Why, he looked and acted no different than many of their own children.

MR. AND MRS. JUSUKE FUKUNAGA
parents of Myles Yutaka, want to express their profound regret for the terrible thing that has happened
and their sorrow for the trouble and anxiety their
son has caused the entire community. And to Mr.
and Mrs. Frederick Jamieson, they offer their deepest
sympathy.

An apology to the people of Hawaii from Myles' parents. *Reprinted from the* Honolulu Star-Bulletin.

Mr. and Mrs. Yusuke Fukunaga were deeply shamed by Myles' actions. At first they couldn't, they wouldn't, believe that their good son was capable of such madness. But as the horrible truth was revealed, as Myles himself confessed, they felt despair and humiliation. Myles had sought to please his parents, and he had failed. The *Star-Bulletin* ran the following announcement the day of the arrest: "Mr. and Mrs. Yusuke Fukunaga, parents of Myles Fukunaga, want to express their profound regret for the terrible thing that has happened, and their sorrow for the trouble and anxiety their son has caused the entire community and to Mr. and Mrs. Frederick Jamieson, they offer their deepest sympathy."

The court system of Hawaii moved swiftly in the case of Myles Fukunaga. On Monday after his arrest, Myles was indicted by the Grand Jury for first degree murder. The population of Honolulu and the newspapers clamored for the death of the young murderer and the Vigilante Corps continued their efforts to revamp Hawaii's laws which required a short waiting period between sentencing and execution; they wanted immediate hanging. By the end of the week Myles had two court appointed attorneys and the trial began on October 3.

During the trial the defense called no witnesses and by October 5, the jury had reached a verdict. Though Myles was a murderer, both the judge, attorneys and jurors were struck by his boyishness, his politeness and his refusal to deny any of his actions. As the verdict of guilty was read, the jurors openly wept and the attorneys had to shield their eyes lest they, too, be accused of being soft-hearted. On October 8, Judge A. Steadman's face was pale and drawn as he hesitantly read the sentence: Myles Fukunaga was to be hanged by the neck until dead. Myles thanked the court and jury for their kindness, courtesy and swift justice.

Though Myles was pleased with the rapidity of his trial and sentencing, the Japanese community which had actively helped to find him was infuriated. The boy had been tried, convicted and sentenced of first degree murder in less than two weeks. A proper defense was not prepared and justice was apparently sacrificed to the demands made by the haole section of the community. Although Myles reiterated constantly "I am not insane," the evidence was overwhelming that this young boy was seriously deranged. But still the court and governor of Hawaii had refused to allow Myles to have psychiatric examination. He had openly confessed, the courts argued; he knew right from wrong; he realized the gravity of his crime and accepted his fate.

The Japanese community, however, would not rest. First a fund was started to eventually send Myles' parents back to Japan to escape the horrible shame they felt in Hawaii. Then numerous leaders in the community signed a petition demanding the retrial of Myles Fukunaga and a proper medical examination of the boy.

The *Hawaii Hochi* under the direction of Fred Makino began to blast the haole newspapers and com-

A meeting of Japanese in Honolulu to discuss the Fukunaga case, November 1929. *Photo courtesy of the Hawaii Hochi.*

munity for the obvious racial overtones in the case. They cited the fact that the way the case was being handled when a Japanese committed a crime was not the way a haole was treated. Just recently the *Hochi* complained, a Japanese taxi cab driver was brutally murdered by a haole who had political influence. The haole was charged with second degree murder, yet there was no uproar of public indignation.

On the Puunene Plantation on Maui a Japanese worker had gasoline poured over him and was burned to death by a white mechanic for apparently no reason. The haole was tried for manslaughter and acquitted. In both cases, the *Hochi* argued, there was no public demand for swift and efficient justice. Hawaii, the Japanese newspaper condemned, had one law for the white man and one law for the non-white man. "What has been sauce for the goose," the *Hochi* wrote, "has not been sauce for the gander."

Believing the treatment of Myles Fukunaga to be a miscarriage of justice, the *Hochi* went further to prove beyond a reasonable doubt that Myles was insane. They cited the ransom letter and the way the boy's body was found. They enlisted the aid of psychologists at the University of Hawaii and Dr. J. C. Thompson, the Senior Medical Officer for the Navy at Pearl Harbor who agreed that Fukunaga was insane. It was reported that Myles' great-aunt had died in an insane asylum, hopelessly mad. On Myles' father's side, it was also rumored, a strain of insanity existed. A cousin of the father who lived in Japan showed marked signs of crazy behavior.

The logic behind the Japanese community's insistence that Myles was insane was very basic. If Myles, an evidently typical and well-behaved Japanese youth were truly sane, then the implication was that any

Japanese could commit such a brutal crime. If he were insane, however, the community's strained image and responsibility for the boy's criminal nature would be absolved. What was at stake wasn't only the fate of Myles Fukunaga, but the image of the Japanese American community.

But the other peoples of Hawaii demanded blood. Any possibility that Myles might be released or escape the gallows could cause serious racial unrest. How would the non-Japanese react to one of their children being murdered by an Oriental and have the courts place the murderer in a hospital at the taxpayer's expense? Public opinion demanded that, "the voice of innocence cries out for revenge."

For one year Myles waited throughout a series of unsuccessful court appeals encouraged and financed by the Japanese community. Myles had had a fair trial, the Supreme Court of the United States finally ruled, and they would not reopen the case. His execution should be carried out as prescribed by law.

As the handsome youth donned the black mask, he was exceedingly calm. The trap door released at 8:10 A.M., November 19, 1929, one year, two months and one day after he had choked the life out of Gill Jamieson. The newspaper reported that "his life was taken by the people of Hawaii to make the lives of others safe." The body hung for 12 minutes before doctors pronounced Myles Fukunaga dead. A Roman Catholic priest who had become Myles' friend and confessor during his year of imprisonment could only utter one word, "Death."

The case of Myles Fukunaga is more than a novel crime case, meant to tantalize the morbidity in each of us. It is more than the sad drama of a young haole boy

"Nothing will prevent us from seeking our ultimate goal."
The grave of Myles Fukunaga. *Photo courtesy of Jerry Y. Fujioka, Light Inc.*

and a Japanese boy who, in their brief moment of encounter, shattered the illusions of racial peace and aloha in Hawaii's community. For the case of Myles Fukunaga also represents some aspects of the past which shaped the history of the Japanese American in Hawaii.

We have seen how Japanese in Hawaii enjoyed a friendly and accepting atmosphere beginning with King Kalakaua and Captain Tōgō. But as the *Hawaii Hochi* pointed out during the Fukunaga case, there was also an atmosphere marked by a dual system of justice, a system based on mistrust and suspicion. Just one week before Myles carried out his tragic plans to bring honor to his parents, an incident occurred which reminded the Japanese that in Hawaii, too, there were times when they were not accepted as full partners in the social system. The McKinley High School baseball team, composed largely of Japanese Americans and returning from a tournament in Japan, were detained at the Immigration Offices despite the fact that their papers were in order and others vouched for their citizenship. To the immigration officials they were Japanese aliens trying to slip into the Islands illegally, not American citizens.

The suspicions and double standard of justice, exposed in the Fukunaga case, represent the same type of darker, and more prejudicial undercurrents of the Hawaiian social system which the Japanese had to encounter in the years before World War II, along with the friendship and equanimity. The plantation system with its manager and servant mentality, the Japanese language school controversy which projected Japanese as un-American, the racial terror and uncertainty of World War II, and in each case the need for the Japanese to "prove themselves," were a series of events which must also be viewed in some measure as the legacy of the past.

The personality and insanity of Myles Fukunaga remain as much an enigma today as they were in 1928. One cannot help but feel the same tinges of remorse and empathy for not only little Gill, but for the young Japanese boy whose life was characterized by one psychiatrist as the "most painful he had ever examined."

For the tragedy involved more than two innocent boys. The tragedy involved the entire community of Hawaii whose social and racial systems were again revealed to be less than always equal. The peoples of Hawaii often stood in different worlds though they shared the same Islands, and when crisis arose the reactions were clearly predictable: the community would demand evidence and the accused would have to prove their good intentions. Indeed, perhaps Myles Fukunaga's actions only represented the results of living a life of second-class citizenship, of being denied those things which others affluently enjoyed. Or perhaps Myles' actions were only the nightmarish fantasies of the mental delusions of his own making. In any case, on that September morning when Myles murdered Gill Jamieson, all of Hawaii was certainly going to reap the whirlwind.

7
Jan Ken Po—
The Island Heritage

"Junk an' a po, I canna show."
"Junk an' a po, I canna show."
"Junk an' a po, I canna show."
The rhythm of Island children playing one of their favorite games can be heard in any playground, backyard or living room.
"Eh, I wanna go first!"
"Why, you like beef?"
"Yeah, you always go first!"
"I neva!"
"Okay you guys, junk an' a po!"
"Junk an' a po, I canna show." The children's clenched fists of their right hand reveal their challenge. Paper (flat open hand) smothers Stone (clenched fist). Stone smashes Scissors (index finger and middle finger in the form of a "V"). Scissors cuts Paper.
"Three out of five, okay?" The left hands count how many times the children win.
"What does 'junk an' a po, I canna show' mean?" you ask them.

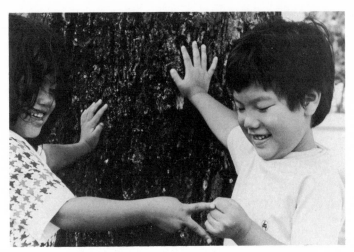

"Junk an' a po, I canna show." *Photo courtesy of Eugene Y. Fujioka, Light Inc.*

"Oh, you know," they answer, "da kine."

"Junk an' a po" has its roots in the Japanese game *Jan Ken Po.* Unlike the Hawaiian version of the simple game which is similar to the mainland game of "Paper and Stone," *Jan Ken Po* is played, at times, with the representation not of objects but of animals. The Frog (a thumb) wins over the old Slug (the little finger). The Slug wins over the Snake (the index finger). The Snake beats the Frog. So beginning in a neutral position of "stone fist," *Jan Ken Po,* the children reveal their animals "all together," *Ai Kono Sho.*

Jan Ken Po, Ai Kono Sho from Japan then, has become in Hawaii "junk an' a po, I canna show." Phonetically they sound very similar, but essentially their meanings are quite different. While the Japanese version is a stylized form of the game with clear definitions and meanings, the version used in Hawaii is a mixture of English, Japanese and pidgin words with the rules adapted to the American game of "Paper and Stone." It is an informal game of gibberish which is used either to pass away an hour or to make a quick decision. But most importantly, it is meant to be fun.

Island children will probably never play the Japanese version of *Jan Ken Po,* nor necessarily should they. They have played "junk an' a po" for decades without knowing its meaning or roots; yet this game, a cultural hybrid, has resolved conflicts, provided answers and offered good entertainment. Even though it is not Japan Japanese, Hawaii Hawaiian or America American, it has served its purposes well.

And if you visit different parts of Hawaii and ask the children how they play "junk an' a po," you will find that each island, each area, plays the game differently. For example, a young man from Ewa Beach, Oahu, said that when he and his neighborhood friends were children they played "Rainbow." Instead of the six beats of "junk an' a po, I canna show," this game only had two, "Rainbow." When his cousins from Honolulu visited during the summer, they would show the Ewa Beach children the "junk an' a po" version. But the Ewa Beach children thought the Honolulu version was too long to simply decide the first team at bat or the first in line—they stuck to their own version, "Rainbow."

On Maui, some children have lengthened the original "junk an' a po" to "Junken a munken a sucka sucka po, Wailuku, Wailuku bum bum sho." Children on the Big Island might change this Maui version slightly: "Junken a munken a sucka sucka po, Wailuku, Wailuku big fat toe." Now these variations certainly are not identical to *Jan Ken Po,* "junk an' a po" or "Rainbow" but they are still a form of the same game which has a small, but highly respected place, in the life of Hawaii.

In many ways the game *Jan Ken Po* is also symbolic of the life and the culture of the Japanese American in Hawaii. It would not be straining a metaphor to say that the history of the Japanese American ethnic group, in relation to all other ethnic groups has been a long and continuous game of *Jan Ken Po*. The future had always been for the Japanese American filled with uncertainty. Which of the undercurrents of Hawaii's social system would gain ascendancy—the friendship established because of events such as Kalakaua's amiability with Japan or the prejudice which would occasionally surface, such as during the Fukunaga case? For how long would that undercurrent be dominant? With what would it be replaced? What could the peoples of Hawaii expect next?

Coming to Hawaii and working on the plantations was a gamble. Could the immigrants find their wealth and status on the plantations working as laborers? Would the environment of Hawaii accept them as brothers or reject them as foes? If they went on strike could they better their lives by beating the sugar planter's oligarchy or would they be broken and subdued?

Trying to make Hawaii their home was a gamble. If they tried to become Americanized would they be accepted by the community or would they be condemned? Could they maintain the necessary ethnic coherency of their community by the perpetuation of things Japanese or would this lead to greater hostility from the community? Would the actions of individuals within the ethnic group always cast a shadow over the entire group demanding a need to prove itself?

Attempting to live within the tenuous balance of Japanese-Hawaiian-American relations was a gamble. If Japan, America and Hawaii had a close and friendly relationship, would the Japanese Americans of Hawaii benefit by being recognized as integral parts of the Island life? If Japan, America and Hawaii were at war, would the Japanese Americans be condemned as the enemy, suspected or even imprisoned?

Emerging from World War II and establishing a firm and respected place in Hawaii was a gamble. Would the postwar community of Hawaii accept Japanese Americans as belonging in the system? Would Japanese Americans always face irrational racial bias? Would other ethnic groups find the Japanese Americans too successful and become resentful of their achieved status?

Jan Ken Po, though, is not a game of high ante poker or Russian roulette. Winner never takes all; there is always another chance, another round of challenge. Although some might feel that Hawaii's history has resembled a conspiracy created by missionaries, sugar planters and Uncle Toms who have sought to control the destiny of the Islands, there was never a guarantee for the future; the law of averages necessitates that no one can win *Jan Ken Po* all the time. A cultural group might have had the upper hand, an inside knowledge of who was going to win. A cultural group might have tried to bind the hands of another so that there would be no competition. But in any case, the contest would go on, during which the social, economic and cultural systems would evolve, and this group, then that, would consider themselves victorious. But always the victory would be temporary. Always those lucky enough to have won would have to retest their luck in another challenge.

In the face of the grand sweep of Hawaii's history, the so-called saga of the Hawaiian Islands which like a novel so often has a dramatic beginning and end, the *Jan Ken Po* interpretation of Hawaii's past seems a little sacrilegious. Rather than Divine predetermination, *Jan Ken Po* suggests that a degree of uncertainty existed and therefore each of the elements of the Island's people had an opportunity to determine the evolutionary path upon which Hawaii's systems would travel. The Hawaii of today was not only designed behind the mahogany doors of a sugar planter's library as the haole pondered the economic world his grandchildren should inherit. It was not only designed in the palace of the Hawaiian kings, the offices of the Big Five, or behind the desk of a Japanese newspaper editor or a Filipino labor leader. The Hawaii in which the Japanese American finds himself and with which he so religiously identifies, is the competitive result of all Hawaii's people attempting to create a home for themselves.

And in the process of establishing a secure home, Hawaii's people have come to share their cultures and their lives. When one speaks about the Japanese, Chinese, Hawaiian or Filipino in Hawaii, one is not talking about separate ethnic units whose communities do not have interactions with each other. Rather one must speak of a shared Island heritage of cultural background and lifestyle. Many of the patterns of life which Japanese Americans follow, their notions of obligation and reciprocal gift-giving, the ideal of beauty and the "good life," can be found among other ethnic groups. And the cultures, languages, and customs of other peoples can be found among the Japanese Americans. Often times, the people of Hawaii as they live their daily lives, are indistinguishable except on the basis of varying racial features.

Of course, much has been written about race relations in Hawaii and the sharing of cultures. Indeed, the image of Hawaii has always been parallel with the idea of the "Melting Pot of the Pacific." Here in these Islands many people from different lands share foods, habits, customs and celebrations, all in an atmosphere of *aloha*.

But most studies have analyzed Hawaii from the viewpoint of groups within the dynamics of the entire community or social system. While this is a necessary and valid approach to the study of Hawaii's racial situation, it overlooks the fact that groups are comprised of individuals. It is on the personal, individualized day-to-day level of living in Hawaii where the different peoples have learned the formula to compatible living. The first frontiers of race relations have been, and will continue to be, the way different peoples approach each other and the manner in which they communicate.

So *Jan Ken Po* is not only symbolic of the relationship between Hawaii's people on the basis of the historical development of ethnic groups as they have attempted to cooperate and compete with each other. It is also symbolic of the person-to-person, daily contact between cultures. Children of all races and social classes find a common meaning and sense of fun in the simple game. Reinterpreted from the Japanese into the local cultural style of "junk an' a po," by its very nature *Jan Ken Po* has come to represent the sharing of cultures in Hawaii.

To understand the process of cultural sharing we must look to the daily interracial communication which takes place between ethnic groups. We must look to the very first frontiers of intercultural dialogue: the rhymes, jokes and stories which people tell each other. The folklore of a people is sometimes neglected as an entertaining but rather trivial aspect of a culture to be studied. But to anyone who lives in Hawaii, the jokes and stories which are told when people "talk story" provide an essential means of communication which frequently transcend any barriers of cultural or racial differences. They become a common denominator of life habits through which tensions can be released and friendships made.

For example, if a Japanese American were to go to a Hawaiian *luau* where he knew only a few people, he would most likely not try to discuss national politics, the price of meat or a Japanese Bon Dance. To bridge the cultural differences between people, he would have a beer and begin to tell a joke, sing a song, or relate a story. Both Japanese Americans and Hawaiians would base their communication on laughing and enjoying themselves together. Indeed, laughter becomes a common human attachment enlivening not only a party but the commonality among Hawaii's people.

At the earliest ages children learn the various rhymes, jokes or saying with which they instinctively relate interracially with other children. To the outside observer some of these childish puns might seem flagrantly evil or prejudicial. They seem to typify the sort of biased slurs and stereotypes which on the mainland produce racial hostilities. But in Hawaii, they are not always considered "bad," Children and adults usually say them not to be degrading of other ethnic groups but as a way to acknowledge and participate in the local culture. The following rhymes have been collected from children and adults and are repeated in the same spirit of common friendship with which they were given:

Porogee, Porogosh,
No wash wash.

One day, two day
Then wash, wash.

Red, White and Blue
Stars over you
Mama said, Papa said
You Pake.

Ahana Kokolele
You broke your Okolele!

Buddhahead digadum
Mello-mello stink plum.

My Pilipines, my Pilipines,
Always pite but no can win.
I love my own my pantaloon,
It's very wide and very long.
I eat potato all the time,
It will make me very strong.

(Sung to the tune of the Philippines National Anthem)

Little Kapena sat on a moena (mat)
Eating his two-finger poi.
He made many dips
Then smacking his lips
Said, "I'll be a pretty fat boy."

(From Hawaiian Mother Goose, *by Emma Doyle and Ethelyn Myhre)*

One thing each ethnic group in Hawaii had to learn was a healthy sense of humor so that they would be able to laugh at each other and not take themselves too seriously. Living on a series of small islands requires a high degree of open friendliness. Therefore, Hawaii's people are not reluctant to poke fun at each other and at themselves by using words which from the mainland standpoint seem derogatory but from the Island perspective seem descriptive or simply funny. "Buddhahead," "Pake," "Kanaka," "Haole Crab," "Bok-Bok," "Porogee Mouth," are just a small sampling of the words which ethnic groups often use in reference to themselves; these words are essential parts of the local Island culture.

Ethnic jokes are another means of relieving tensions between people and bridging cultures on the personal level. The jokes told among Island people are again an example of the process which residents of Hawaii have learned: slight self-deprecation for the sake of group harmony. By being the brunt of a joke, each ethnic group in effect "humbles" itself; no one is so important, so significant that they can't be made fun of. No group is free from the light gibes or puns which accompany this aspect of Hawaii's humor. Again, it is expected that the listener will not find these jokes racially derogatory or insulting, but good-natured fun.

The following sample of jokes are those told most often by Island people and entertainers. Many times mainland tourists will be appalled at the kinds of jokes Don Ho, Zulu or the Society of Seven will tell during their acts, especially when they refer to haoles. But Island people cannot appreciate such criticism because this style of humor is not meant to insult, but to reaffirm that one shares in the "local" culture.

Once, there was a great Hawaiian King who ruled all the Hawaiian Islands. He lived in a large grass shack that was surrounded by a wide moat containing sharks.

He also had a very beautiful daughter that all the Hawaiian men wished they could marry.

As the years went by, the Hawaiian King was getting too old to carry the burden of ruling a kingdom that consisted of seven islands. He wanted to find someone strong who might be willing to take his place. So he called all the men of all the islands together and told them that he would grant any wish to the first one who swam across the moat safely.

As soon as the men heard this, over half of them jumped into the water. But the sharks got them all before they even got half way. After seeing this the rest of the men hesitantly tried one by one, but none of them made it across.

After two hours had gone by, the king began to grow tired and finally fell asleep. All of a sudden there was a big splash and the king woke up to see a great big Hawaiian trying to make it across. Surprisingly, he was successful.

The king ran up to him and said, "What is it that you want? Would you like to marry my daughter and rule my kingdom?"

"No!" answered the big Hawaiian. "I like get that damn haole that went push me into the water!"

There were three boys, one Chinese, one Japanese and one Hawaiian playing together. The Chinese boy said, "When I grow up I am going to be an astronaut and fly to Mars." Then the Japanese boy said, "I am going to be an astronaut too, but I am going to Mercury."

Then the Hawaiian boy said, "When I grow up I am going to be an astronaut too, but I am going to be the most famous astronaut of all. I am going to the sun!"

The other two boys started to laugh. The Hawaiian boy asked, "Why are you laughing?"

The Japanese boy answered, "Why, as soon as you get near the sun, it will be so hot that you'll burn up."

"You think me stupid or what?" the Hawaiian boy said. "I going nighttime!"

There was a Filipino scientist who wished to become famous by training a cockroach. He started by first letting a cockroach run down a straight runway and pass a line. The first attempt was a great success as the cockroach passed the finish line with ease.

With great jubilation, the Filipino scientist decided to cut two legs off the cockroach to see just how smart it was. With some struggle, the cockroach again passed the finish line. "This cockroach will make me rich," the scientist thought to himself, "it's so smart!"

Then the Filipino scientist removed two more legs and with much effort the cockroach again passed the finish line. The scientist was flabbergasted with the cockroach's intelligence.

Finally he cut off the last two legs of the cockroach. But when he said "Run cockroach," the cockroach just didn't move. Dejectedly the Filipino scientist recorded in his experiment book, "After cutting off all of its legs, the cockroach became deaf."

There were two men in a bar, one Kanaka and one haole. The haole guy started to act wise, so the Kanaka said "Step outside, brah." BOOM! The Kanaka on the ground! The haole he say, "Karate from Japan."

They went back into the bar, the haole guy still acting wise, so the Kanaka say "Eh, step outside." BOOM!

BOOM! The Kanaka on the ground again and the haole say "Kung Fu from China."

So they went back into the bar and again the haole act wise. So the Kanaka say "Step outside." BOOM! BOOM! BOOM! The haole guy on the ground and the Kanaka say, "Crowbar from Sears."

A Chinese, a Portuguese and a Japanese are in a small boat together fishing in the ocean. But the boat sprung a leak and they all drowned. The Chinese had so many coins in his pocket he sank. The Portuguese couldn't keep his mouth shut so he swallowed too much water and drowned. And the Japanese guy, he didn't know what to do so he copied the other two.

This Portuguese guy, Manuel, worked in the woods cutting trees everyday. But he could cut only three trees a day with his saw.

So Manuel went into town to the store and said to the Japanese owner, "Eh, I only cut three trees a day with dis saw. You can give me somtin' betta?"

The Japanese man gave Manuel a new gasoline chain saw and Manuel went back home. But the next day he again could only cut three trees. So he goes back to the Japanese man and says, "Eh, dis saw you wen give me no work; I cut only three trees one day with dis."

So the Japanese man took the chain saw, gave it a pull with the rope and it started up, "Rooo—ar."

"Eh," Manuel said, "What dat noise?"

These jokes are repeated here because in the context of living in Hawaii, of being a "Japanee" in Hawaii, they reveal many dimensions of the intercultural nature of the Islands. Only in Hawaii can this type of joke be innocently enjoyed without stirring the wrath of the ethnic groups involved. They are told as a way to facilitate communication between the races by easing tensions and establishing an atmosphere of good humor. Indeed, through humor, the Japanese American and Hawaii's other people are confirming their human relationships.

Another way in which the people of Hawaii share culture is through the stories or legends which are told among men, women and children. The contents of the stories are often humorous, sometimes extraordinary and perhaps frightening, but they are always meant to be entertaining. At any rate, whenever a story is being told you can rest assured that everyone will be listening intently. They will be conjuring in their minds the settings and scenes which are so familiar to anyone who has been raised in Hawaii and shares in the local culture.

The following three stories are but a small sampling of the tales which one hears among friends, relatives, or acquaintances. They are told by a Japanese-Hawaiian who in many ways, as revealed in his stories, typifies the theme of *Jan Ken Po*—not Japanese, Hawaiian or American, but a mixture of all. His identity and culture are fused with the identity and the cultures of Hawaii. Unfortunately, the written word loses a lot of the meanings that can be transmitted through oral communication. But these stories, which are told with a mixture of pidgin and standard English, represent the type of warm human feeling that people share when "talking story."

I had spent quite a long time in Tripler Hospital recuperating from the Korean War in 1952, so I made a lot of friends there, mostly Japanese. Let me tell you that we had a real close friendship. We used to go downtown, many without leg, many can't see. I was one of the fortunate ones because I had braces. So we used to come to town and we would get into fights with whole-bodied men. But we had our own art, our own particular ways. They don't last too long. We would just mobilize!

But anyways you know Orientals are scary; they get awful scared of something spiritual like spooks and things like that. One day we were talking about the supernatural. We heard some stories about the Nuuanu Pali. They say if you take pork on the ol' Pali road, if you take raw pork up to that mountain at the stroke of twelve, you'll neva get to seeing that pork eva again. These people say that they literally see the pork fly away from the package in the trunk or on the seat. So they wanted to try it out. But I didn't want to go. I thought it was full of nonsense. And if it wasn't, I wasn't about to try it. Let me tell you, I wasn't stupid, you know.

So about four of those guys went up. But how they did it was kind of funny because they were real scared. They bought a big porkchop, and they took it up there. Two guys was in the back and two guys in the front. They had a stick fastened on to the meat. And they had the stick protruding out of the car with the window rolled up holding it in place. So the meat is out, hanging on the stick, and they are all in there looking at it. They can see the meat as they shine the light. So they went up there just on the stroke of twelve, at Nuuanu Pali. And by golly, that meat disappeared. It actually disappeared. They haul tail out of there, boy! They disappeared, let me tell you. The driver he dropped everybody off and then he went home.

They tol' me the story the next day and man did I laugh. They were really scared. The last guy who was driving, he had to take one of those four guys with him because he wouldn't drive home himself. But then the next day, they woke up; the sun was shining. Everything was through, and they were having breakfast. They were really excited about what had happened the night before. But when the guy got into his car that morning, lo and behold, you know on the running board? There was a stinking piece of meat with all kine of flies on it! What a let down! Oh boy, man was that funny. He said "Wat dose flies dere?" And there was a ol' rotten piece of meat!

I don't know if you've encountered this before but it's unbelievable. There was this Japanese fellow and he and I roomed in one studio apartment and we slept on one bed. One night, we both were in bed and I was facing away from the door. As I was sleeping I was surprised to see a woman looking at my back right from the doorway, you know? Looking right down at me! So I opened my eyes and looked at her. Yeah, there shouldn't be anybody in this apartment except my friend and I. Now if she was a young woman then that's something else you know, but she was an old lady. And I didn't care too much for that! So I opened my eyes, and this is fact, I swear, that woman was still there, still there! But I didn't turn around. I opened my eyes and I seen her at the door.

Alright, my friend was fast asleep and let me tell you again that Japanese bunch of scarecrows. They really are, you know. So I talked to myself, "she's there looking at me, my eyes is open; I am awake and she's still there. I'm going to turn around right now." So I turned around and there weren't anyone, but then there was a shadow on the ceiling.

I woke up my buddy and I told him the story and oh, he got awful scared. I mean really scared. He was a short little Japanese guy but we were all men. We were going to college under the GI bill so we were all men. And that guy was so scared, he snuggled up close to me like we were nuts or something. I told him the best thing we could do was, my old Hawaiian ancestors says to sprinkle salt in the room to get away all that evil spirit, you know. Eh, let me tell you, we almost used the whole salt. If anything alive in that room, boy they would have ate that salt and sure got killed!

This is a true story that happened long time ago. I come from way over in the boondocks. I was raised on a ranch; horses, cattle, that was my life. I neva loved anything mo' betta than a horse and during my life I had about five horses. And we had dogs galore and my favorite pastime when I was a youngster was to go hunt. Lots of guys have sports, well my sport was hunting. On that land, there's thousands and thousands of acre of this pasture land and forest and my grandfather happened to be the manager of the ranch.

And you know, those Japanese cowboys, they're really good. They would really show up those Texas cowboys. But they have their short stubby legs sticking out of the horse. The horses have a big belly, and usually the cowboys in the movies have their legs hanging down along side, you know. But not these Japanese cowboys. They can't hang their legs because they are so short so they harig out like a "V." And they can't use spurs. You know spurs, you have to dig into the rib. But their feet stick out so much that if they try to kick, they can't reach the skin. So dey use whip. These Japanese cowboys always use whip. So the horses that are given to them don't know what it's like to be kicked by spurs!

Well on this ranch when I was a young boy we had to go out and hunt wild dogs. There hundreds of dogs in the mountain forest and they kill the animals, the beef, you know the young calves, and different kine of game. So we try to kill those animals, those wild dogs. They're vicious! Our domestic dogs we train to hunt animals. When we go up in the forest let's say, to hunt for pigs or wild cattle and we approach these wild dogs, we don't eva get off the horse. They'll attack us real easy. But on many many occasions, I have neva yet seen a wild dog win from a fight among domestic dogs and wild dogs. It's very unusual because those wild dogs are very lanky and mean, you know. They always killing for meat. But I don't think they kill for just the joy of killing, just because they want to kill. Whereas domestic dogs they have joy of killing. We train those domestic dogs to kill cattle. But they know what kind of cattle to attack and what kind we don't attack. We train them to kill goats, sheep, wild pigs and oh all kinds of animals. So everytime they encounter these wild dogs, these wild dogs are beaten off by these domestic dogs. Can you imagine that, it's hard to believe eh? Usually you think that the wild dogs superior but the domestic dogs mo' superior and they really beat the daylights out of the dogs. So many get killed by the domestic dogs. And if you ever see the domestic dogs fight, you neva know how vicious they are.

The story of this whole thing happened, oh way back when I was living on my grandfather's ranch. But I was too young to rememba. Now my grandfather one day, he and all his cowboys went up to do some branding. Oh, this was a vast land and there was a section where all the cattle could be put together and they would weed out all the young ones. Then they would put a brand on them, these calves. And it was on this day when my grandfather went up into that corral. He seen this wild mother dog and oh that mother dog came up to him.

They know about a gun you know, and so my father took out his 30-30. Everybody have a 30-30 on their horse. My grandfather whip out that 30-30 and that dog haul. But my grandfather's a top-notch shooter, you know. I mean that guy, nobody can eva beat him to shoot. And he had those old 30-30 that has this octagon shaped barrel. Oh you can't find those guns. And he killed that mother dog. And right in that area where that mother dog was, under a fallen hollow tree, had a litter of two puppies. Two very young puppies. Just about a couple o' days ol' perhaps. One was black and the other was red. So he had compassion over those two mountain dogs. After branding he brought home the dogs and started to feed them. Neva has he done this before. He started to feed these wild dogs. And he called one Red and the other one Jackie.

On the ranch being that my grandfather was the manager, no other cowboy can have dogs because then there will be too many dogs. So he had all the dogs and he had about a dozen or fifteen of those dogs. You know he watches and trains those dogs personally. Now when he takes a dog out to hunt fo' cattle or fo' pig and if the dog goes fo' the hind leg, he'll get rid of the dog by shooting him. Just by watching them on the first attempt, no second chance. And many a times he will shoot the dog right there. After raising them up, you know almost to a year old. But if they go for the nose or the ear then he keeps the dog. So these one dozen dogs, or whatever, they are all trained to go for the head. And that's the worst—headhunters is what they call it. The dogs don't last too long because the only defense of the wild animal's the head with the sharp razor blade tusk. But that's the only way he trains his dogs, not to harm the meat. Now you get dat?

So the dogs have to take their chances with the tusks, the jaws. So anyhow, those two dogs without any worries, they always go for the head. They real, real good dogs. So as a year or two went by, these two wild dogs, Jackie and Red, became very, very close to my grandfather. These other domestic dogs neva had a chance to beat these two dogs. And so every time when my grandfather goes out, these two dogs go with him. And no other two dogs would be able to go with them. They got no chance. These dogs were jus' mean! Wicked hunters! I mean they could smell a pig a mile away. They could track a footstep from yesterday and find the pig. I don't know how in the world that comes about, but maybe it is in their hunting blood, you know? I don't know how to explain that.

But then I came into the picture because I got to really know those dogs. We would hunt cattle and oh my goodness! I have neva seen any dog mo' controlled. I think they have a mind of their own. They can knock down a bull at any time by just hitting their vital spots, you understand? And the vital spots happens to be their nose and in the backside. If they go for any other part the bull would just gnaw them to death. From a far distance the bull would always charge the dogs; the dogs neva charge the bull, yeah? The other dogs, the bull charges and they bark and run away, and that's how it goes. But these two dogs they wait for this bull. The two dogs wait on the side and when the bull comes it comes fo' one. And as soon as the bull reaches maybe five feet away, they'll leap towards the bull! And it always happen that they neva miss. If they miss they dead. Yeah! The fangs goes right into the nose, oh my goodness! The big monstrous bull, about a ton and a half, fell! He jus' paralyzed! "Murr," like dat. And the other one just grr--ab 'em in the back! So we put the rope around the bull's horns and tie it against the tree. And then we go for another one since we get about $50 a bull. That's how we make our side money.

Oh, those dogs real fantastic dogs. Anyhow, one day something happened and those two dogs didn't come home. So my grandfather went around looking for the dogs and called them. He called all over the spots where they like. Another day and another day and so he got panicky. So he thought, "well perhaps they went goat hunting." And there's a lot of caves. Big caves you know, you could put a house in it. And he think that perhaps those two dogs chase a goat and fell in a cave. And so right after work my grandfather asked fo' volunteers. They know that these two dogs among all the other dogs will give them meat fo' the whole ranch at any time, you know. So they all volunteer after work to go look fo' the dogs. I tell you that went on fo' days and went into weeks. . . . Finally half of the crew gave up. But my grandfather jus' wouldn't give up. He planned where they would look, here to here. He mapped it all out, you know? So it was finally jus' him and a few other guys and they came across on this cave and they looked over, and sure enough, Jackie and Red was in there. Well, what was remaining of Red. What happened was they chase the goat and the goat fell in the cave as my grandfather guessed. And those dogs followed right after. Red got killed, since it was about a twenty-five foot fall. So how Jackie survived all that three or four weeks, was by eating the goat first. Then he had no choice but to eat his brother. So it was just the remains of Red. And when my grandfather got a hold of him, oh that dog was jus' near death. Jus' bones.

Now to tell you how fantastic Jackie is, let me tell you how we go hunting. I am a teenager now, maybe 12 years old. And like I said I love to hunt. So after school perhaps my friends and I take Jackie and go hunt goats. And this is how Jackie hunts the goat. Our ranch is right on a hill and there's miles and miles of plateau. Those goats you can see them from the ocean coming up. So we would watch and if they come up enough so that I can go for a mile or two, there's all lava rocks you know, if they come up that high then I'll go hunt. We sell a goat about 5 dollas a goat. So we take Jackie, and Jackie goes ahead. These goats are about 75 yards away and there's a herd of them there. So we let Jackie go. And Jackie, he doesn't do like all the domestic dogs! He doesn't jus' run into the pile and then catch the weakest because they the last in the bunch. He doesn't do that.

First of all he studies the wind, eh? And if the wind is blowing this way, he doesn't go toward the goat. He maneuvers himself around so that the wind will be in front of him, right? And then he works his way up towards the goat. And on many, many occasions, the goat will not know he's there. Goats are funny, you know. You see, goats when there is a herd there's always a boss in this herd. And that boss always the biggest, with biggest horns. He is always on the hill and he watches over his flock. He stay there jus' like one statue! On that hill jus' seeing, jus' watching fo' enemies. Jackie knows this! So he doesn't watch for the fattest of the herd, he's watching that billy on the hill, eh? As long as that billy is not looking his way, he'll sneak a little mo'. But soon as that billy looks his way, he stop. And the only thing you can see from him is his ear. Yeah? His ear is jus' flapping like dat, okay? These billies, they go in shifts. This billy stays up fo' about half hour, then he goes down. And another billy goes up to that same spot. That's when Jackie really make his move. So when that other billy is coming up he hauls. He really hauls! Oh, this way, this way, this way. Let me tell you, and this is the Gospel truth. Those animals are eating right with him. And he's jus' there. He's not looking up, his jaws are straight on the ground. And he's jus' waiting. So these goats come right up to him, brush aside, walk over him. Yeah? They do everything. When they are eating right by him, then he grabs a hold of the ear and those goats starts to run! That's when my friend and I we haul because if we don't get there, the goat will lose his ear. Then the price drops, you see. So he grabs that ear and we take off over there and catch that goat. Usually it's a young billy or a mother; we train them that way. Neva a baby or a big billy. We don't like big billys; they smell! Now we neva trained Jackie to do that; he does it on his own. But then we always teach him what kine goat we want.

The city where I come from has about 1,500 people, but that's a big town where I come from. I come from way in the sticks, you see. But in the city, that's where we go to school. Early in the morning, jus' before day-break we have to walk up from our ranch and we go to the main road to catch the bus. Leading to the main road is a stone wall, you know the old-fashioned kine about five feet high. Well one time, my cousin got nasty with Jackie. Well, Jackie is a dog that neva, neva forgets. Anyways, it takes a while before he forgets. I think he spanked Jackie, and Jackie wouldn't forgive him. For the next two weeks, you know what my cousin had to do? He had to walk on that stone wall to get to the road. Now Jackie could get on that stone wall, but jus' to punish him for what he did, he would jus' follow my cousin. We would walk along the side of the wall, all of us walking along with Jackie, but Jackie's eyes always on my cousin. Oh he's crying, crying the first couple of days. Oh he's cry baby. He would plead to Jackie but Jackie would "graaa" and grab him again. And so my cousin would climb back up on the wall and he'd say "Hold the dog." But we wouldn't hold the dog, and we'd say "It's good for you." And Jackie would follow him right up to the road, then we hold Jackie and my cousin would run into the bus. We would let Jackie go and he would go home. Four-thirty, I swear Jackie is over there again. He is on the main road waiting for the bus. Really! So we hold Jackie, my cousin gets on the wall. He just panics. Everyday he hopes Jackie forgive and forget him, you know. But Jackie's right there. That went on for a couple of weeks until Jackie forgot about it.

Now my grandfather used to scold me and I mean I

could hardly breathe I would be crying. And this is not a spank, it's a tongue lashing. You get awful upset, maybe your father scolded you like that. I would get awful hurt, just so sad. But then I neva expected it to happen to Jackie. He tongue lashed Jackie one day and I tell you that dog he put his tail underneath him and jus' walked away. That evening my grandfather went to feed Jackie, but Jackie wasn't there. Oh, he called Jackie, called Jackie, called Jackie. But he forgot that he tongue lashed him. Eh, all that night, the next morning he figured Jackie was going to be home, but Jackie not there. Then he knew why Jackie not there, because he tongue lash him. But he couldn't figure out where Jackie was. Another day passed by, another day. Eh, he got awful worried. What had Jackie done now? Where did he go? Would he walk away and neva come back? That dog might neva had come back, he was so hurt. Finally my grandfather said "I think I know where Jackie is."

So he goes by himself back to the same corral where he first found Jackie. Under the same tree, under the same stump, Jackie was there. When he got hurt, he decided to go back to the place of his birth. For three days he stayed there. So my grandfather went up to him under that stump and he begged forgiveness, just like Jackie one human bein'! Crazy man. Ah, all of us was awful happy when my grandfather came back and Jackie was waggin his tail, comin' home!

You know a dog has a certain life span, I think 15 years. Well Jackie lived right up very close to those 15 years. These domestic dogs, as the years went by, these dogs don't last too long, maybe a year or two and then they die. Always by a pig or bull. These dogs always change, and the new dogs that they train always try to be leader of the pack. And Jackie always has to fight, give um' lickin! Well it went on an' on an' on an' always he was the leader of the pack. All the time, until in the way later years. Jackie got to the point where he got really old. I remember one time we went hunting and he did the same thing he has done all that many years. He would do everything that he was supposed to do, and he would grab the ear and the goat keep runnin away, keep runnin away! Jackie don't have no teeth! No teeth! He's so old he lost all his teeth. He gummed the ear. The goat would jus' run away with all that saliva in that ear.

Anyhow, he died a real veteran of all hunting dogs. I neva seen any dog like dat. But how he died was, one of these young dogs, and it was a big one, wanted to take over the pack. I was home in the parlor, and I could always hear Jackie's bark among all other dogs. He had a certain bark or growl. So he started to bark and growl and I knew Jackie was attempting to protect his reign. So when I went out there, the young dog started to fight with Jackie, and Jackie did his very best to fight back. And then the other dogs piled on Jackie because they wanted a new leader, you know. So there was about six dogs on Jackie and he died instantly right there.

Most dogs when they die, we would throw down the hill. That's what my grandfather does. But with Jackie, he had a decent burial. . . . That dog was somtin' else.

This story and the others have been repeated here not because they are overly-dramatic, suspenseful or classical but because they are typical of the tales which the people of Hawaii relate to one another; they are representative of the narratives which emerge from day-to-day living on the Islands. "Talking story" is not only meant to dramatize events, to get a big laugh or to get applause, but is also often intended to reaffirm the cultural and life backgrounds which people share. Whether talking about the supernatural, hunting, relatives or oneself, the referent is always the human nature of life as it is lived in Hawaii. Whether the story is a little confusing, a little long, a little silly, it doesn't matter; the story is always real. It always reflects the common life of a people.

Jan Ken Po, thus, becomes very symbolic in understanding the process of Hawaii's common identity among ethnic groups. The most important result of living in close proximity, of exchanging stories, jokes and lifestyles is that diverse races and cultures have learned to relate to each other and live in relative harmony to a degree unprecedented anywhere else in the United States. Only in Hawaii have a people as varied as the Hawaiian, Japanese, Filipino, haole, Chinese, Korean, Puerto Rican and Portuguese been able to share language, humor, foods, customs and common respect in such a remarkable way. Though this aspect of the Island's cultural sharing is far from complete, it is continually at work to create a common identity for all those who call Hawaii home. And just as in the game of *Jan Ken Po,* a degree of uncertainty and optimism remains in what this identity will involve in the future. For tomorrow another toss of the fingers will reveal another facet, another experience to be lived and understood.

Epilogue

The cultural identity of Hawaii's Japanese Americans is a product of many factors, some subtle and some obvious. As we have seen, within the framework of parents, siblings and relatives, Japanese Americans learn a system of values essential to their primary referent group, the family. They learn that they are responsible not only for themselves but for the image which their actions cast upon the good name of their parents and ancestors. They learn that more important than individual freedom is the filial piety and love which the family deserves.

In addition, the Japanese Americans' identity is influenced by notions of beauty and sex which prevail in their community. What they see when they look into a mirror and when they look at their mates influence their attitudes toward love. They learn that the images and stereotypes which are created for their ethnic group, as well as other groups, may affect their self-identification but are not wholly representative or accurate.

Other factors which help to define the identity of

Japanese Americans are their peer group relations. Among their community of friends Japanese Americans learn the system of obligation which enhances their human relationships. They learn that to give or reciprocate help and energy to others is a necessary and fundamental way of life.

Finally, the identity of modern Japanese Americans of Hawaii has been influenced by the historical factors of interethnic contacts. Because of the friendly and cordial atmosphere which was often created for them, Japanese Americans were able to identify with Hawaii as their home. Because the people of Hawaii were able to acknowledge Japanese Americans as neighbors, they became an integral part of the Island society. But because of a past which also had elements of prejudice and hostility, Japanese Americans learned that much had to be done before Hawaii could truly become their home. They learned that social justice required an open and honest communication between ethnic groups which could create a secure environment for their children.

And so through the elements of family, sexual images, peer groups, a past with undercurrents of friendship and hostility, the Japanese Americans' identity has come to be a cultural mixture not unlike the simple game of *Jan Ken Po*. Cultural elements of Japan, America and Hawaii, uniquely shared, are the mainstays of their lives.

It is not surprising, then, that a great many Japanese Americans have come to identify themselves primarily with Hawaii and only secondarily with being a Japanese American. Even the usage of the term Japanese American is sometimes criticized as not being accurate. "I am a Hawaiian," many a Japanese, Chinese, Filipino and

Children of Hawaii, circa 1920. Photo courtesy of the Hawaii State Archives.

haole will insist. The whole series of sociological tests social scientists use to determine the acculturation of Japanese Americans in Hawaii become meaningless when confronted with the simple fact that perhaps the Island culture is the predominant one and perhaps eventually the cultural distinctions which remain between ethnic groups will be accented by a common lifestyle and identity.

What the nature of this Island culture will be in the future remains the final and most intriguing question for this book, for Japanese Americans and all of Hawaii's people. Can the methods of living on these small islands which the people of Hawaii have developed over the course of 200 years, marked with friendship and *aloha,* be understood and exported? Can the island culture be made viable and enduring in the face of the future pressures on Hawaii's community? Can people on the mainland learn to develop a style of living which is also marked by a common respect and friendliness for varied peoples and cultures? Indeed, is there a pattern of life in Hawaii that possibly could be transplanted to world situations which daily appear to suffer from intercultural hostilities?

Needless to say, the Hawaii in which we all want to live will exploit the undercurrents of friendliness to its fullest—with each culture, each ethnic group finding those threads from their lifestyles which could be woven with other ethnic groups into a durable fabric of Island living. For example, those people who have been influenced by the Polynesian heritage must continue to teach the values of good humor and the techniques for avoiding self-defeating quarrels. Living on a small island where there is little opportunity to avoid those with whom one is at conflict necessitates an arrangement whereby people can resolve their difficulties with compatibility. In addition, the Polynesian culture offers a respect of nature which is obviously so critically needed if wise decisions concerning Hawaii's economic and social development are to be sound and beneficial for all.

Those who are of Asian heritage must be able to preserve and transmit to others some of the basic values of obligation and cohesive family strength which enhance Hawaii's stable and self-sustaining environment. If the values of obligation to parents could be taught, then perhaps many of the problems which confront the aged in our society could be placed in saner perspective. If obligation to friends and community could be instilled, then perhaps many of the problems of crime, pollution and cultural discrimination could be improved. And if more of our public officials felt a close moral obligation to the people, then perhaps many of the forces on the national and local levels which have led to corruption and a disenfranchisement of the citizenry's rights and powers could be reversed. If the Polynesian, Asian and American cultures could be more viably combined and employed in mutually creative roles, then certainly not only Hawaii, but all those interested in alleviating human predicaments, would benefit.

The Hawaiian, the Chinese, the Filipino, the haole, the Puerto Rican, the Portuguese, the Samoan, the Korean, the Japanese—all Americans who call Hawaii their home, play a valuable part in contributing to the future. There need be no more looking to the past to lament that this or that has already been predetermined. There need be no more looking to the mainland or one's ancestral land for a mirror of an identity which lies with the Islands. We must appreciate ourselves and our cultural lifestyles so that we can know what is worthwhile and beneficial to the development of an even richer culture for all people. And we must do these things in the spirit of our Island heritage. We must work toward providing an example of how human beings can live in peace together.

A Note on Sources

The story "Marriage in Heaven," by Tsuneichi Yamamoto related in Chapter Three, can be found in the *Honolulu Star-Bulletin,* November 18, 1967, B-12.

Sources used for Chapter Five include William N. Armstrong's *Around the World With A King* (New York, 1904); R. S. Kuykendall's *The Hawaiian Kingdom* (Honolulu, 1967); United Japanese Society of Hawaii's *A History of Japanese in Hawaii* (Honolulu, 1971); Ernest K. Wakukawa's *A History of the Japanese People in Hawaii* (Honolulu, 1938); the *Daily Pacific Commercial Advertiser,* issues from January to April 1881 and February 1885; and the article "A Royal Romance," in *Pacific Family Graphic,* Vol. II, No. 3, April 1953, p. 2, 26–31.

Sources used in Chapter Six include Lockwood Myrick's *An Open Letter to Governor Wallace R. Farrington on Fukunaga's Insanity* (Honolulu, 1928), and the issues of the *Honolulu Advertiser, Honolulu Star-Bulletin, Hilo Tribune,* and *Hawaii Hochi* from the months September to October 1928 and November 1929.

A description of the Japanese game *Jan Ken Po* and its English translation comes from an interview with Toraki Kimura in Genie Pitchford's column "Today's Pitch," in the April 9, 1953 edition of the *Honolulu Advertiser.*

Glossary

banzai Japanese cheers traditionally given at weddings and other joyous occasions

chi-chi Japanese term used in the Islands to refer to breasts

daikon Japanese radish

Dai Nippon Great Japan

giri Japanese term for obligation

goza Japanese woven straw mats

haole Hawaiian term for Caucasian; foreigner

Hawaii Ponoi Originally the Hawaiian National Anthem, now the official State Song; composed by King Kalakaua

hibachi Japanese portable charcoal brazier

Issei First generation immigrant Japanese

kamaaina Long-term resident of Hawaii

Ken Geographic division in Japan; a prefecture

kōden Japanese term for an obituary gift; a return for an obituary gift

Kotonk Japanese American from the mainland U.S.

local Term used to describe long-term residents generally of non-haole origin; includes kamaaina haoles

luau Hawaiian feast

luna Hawaiian term for foreman or working boss widely used on Hawaii's sugar plantations

mahu Hawaiian term for homosexual; transvestite

malihini Relative newcomer to Hawaii

Meiji Era The period of Japanese Emperor Meiji's ascendency, 1868–1912

mochi Japanese rice cake

musubi Japanese rice ball

namasu Japanese dish of raw fish and vegetables seasoned with vinegar

nasubi Japanese term for eggplant

nori Japanese seaweed prepared in various forms; dried, shredded, seasoned or in paste

Nisei Second generation Japanese American

nishime Japanese dish of vegetable and meat steamed in soy sauce

ogo Edible seaweed commonly found on Hawaiian shores

ogo-namasu Japanese dish of seaweed and fish seasoned with vinegar

okazu stand Japanese delicatessen

pidgin English The Island dialect which is influenced by a mixture of the languages of various ethnic groups in Hawaii

Punahou Exclusive private school in Honolulu

pupu Plates of hot or cold hors d'oeuvres usually served with drinks

sake Japanese rice wine

Sansei Third generation Japanese American

sashimi Japanese dish of raw fish

senbetsu Japanese term for a parting or farewell gift

sushi Japanese preparation of vinegared rice made with fish and other ingredients

takuan Japanese pickled radish

tempura Japanese dish of seafood and/or vegetables deep fried

Tenjiku Heavenly Place; Japanese term for India synonymous with the sacred home of Buddha which was believed to be the destination of man

teriyaki Japanese dish of meat, poultry or fish marinated with soy sauce

ume Japanese preserved plums

Yonsei Fourth generation Japanese American

⅄ Production Notes

This book was designed by Roger J. Eggers and typeset on the Unified Composing System by the design and production staff of The University Press of Hawaii.

The text typeface is California and the display typeface is Korinna.

Offset presswork and binding were done by Halliday Lithograph. Text paper is Glatfelter P & S Offset, basis 55.